SOUTH YORKSHIRE

GEOFFREY HOWSE

SUTTON PUBLISHING

Sutton Publishing Limited
Phoenix Mill · Thrupp · Stroud
Gloucestershire · GL5 2BU

First published 2007

Copyright © Geoffrey Howse, 2007

Title page photograph: On the way to the
races. An early Edwardian postcard
showing people of all classes arriving at
Doncaster Racecourse on Town Moor.
(*Chris Sharp of Old Barnsley*)

British Library Cataloguing in Publication Data
A catalogue record for this book is available from the
British Library.

ISBN 978-0-7509-4658-2

Typeset in 10.5/13.5 Photina.
Typesetting and origination by
Sutton Publishing Limited.
Printed and bound in England.

This book is dedicated to the memory of my cousin Robert Nelder
14 March 1957 – 27 June 2006

An early twentieth-century postcard of Barnsley Aqueduct at Hoyle Mill, demolished in 1954.
(*Brian Elliott collection*)

CONTENTS

An early twentieth-century postcard of the Norman Conisborough Castle, a jewel in South Yorkshire's crown, considered one of the finest survivals in the whole of Europe. *(Brian Elliott collection)*

INTRODUCTION

Long before the creation in 1974 of the short-lived but little missed South Yorkshire County Council, there had been an area within the West Riding referred to as South Yorkshire. There has never been a South Riding – except in the eponymous work of fiction by Winifred Holtby, published in 1936, the year after her death – because riding means 'a third part of', and historically Yorkshire's Ridings have been the East, North and West. I don't mind this portion of the West Riding being known as South Yorkshire, as I remember as a Cub Scout in the early 1960s having a black and silver triangular badge sewn on one arm of my bottle-green jersey, proudly proclaiming the words 'South Yorkshire'. But we all knew we were still part of the West Riding – and in my eyes still are, even though, from an administrative point of view, the Ridings no longer exist. I abhor the idea, which seemed to have gained credence once South Yorkshire County Council was created, that this little enclave was somehow once severed from the West Riding itself. Along with many other Yorkshiremen, I steadfastly refused to accept this act of administrative vandalism – much as did those true Englishmen who objected when it was announced they should be become part of a county known as Humberside, Avon or, worse still, the hideously named West Midlands. South Yorkshire, however, exists as a clearly defined geographical area and it would be very difficult to argue with that.

Although for over thirty years my principal residence has been in London, my family home has remained in Yorkshire, in that part of the county known as South Yorkshire. I still deem it to be part of the West Riding, perhaps more so, as one of my relations, Sir Thomas Tomlinson, was Chairman of West Riding County Council (1946–9 and 1952–5). And I nurture hopes that somehow good sense will prevail and the disastrous changes made to local and regional government in 1974 will soon be reversed.

South Yorkshire is divided into four major conurbations: the metropolitan boroughs of Barnsley, Doncaster, Rotherham and Sheffield. These principal towns and cities all have a rich history, but many smaller towns and villages within South Yorkshire have a more interesting history, in some cases of far greater significance in the affairs of the entire country, not just their own locality and the old county of Yorkshire. The loss of identity exacerbated by the creation of the metropolitan boroughs should not be under-estimated. There is nothing more galling, when one is away from Yorkshire, than to overhear the following conversation: 'Where do you come from?' The reply is 'Doncaster' or 'Barnsley'. It then turns out that the person from Doncaster comes from Tickhill, a historic market town with ancient origins, situated 7 miles south of Doncaster; and the person from Barnsley in fact comes from Skiers Hall, a hamlet in the old township of Hoyland, closer to Rotherham than Barnsley. Have these people no pride? It does make one wonder.

For this book I have chosen images from a wide range of places throughout South Yorkshire. Inevitably, areas of which there are more interesting photographs receive greater coverage than others. The Fitzwilliam (Wentworth) Estates feature frequently because together they form by far the largest estate in South Yorkshire and include towns, villages and hamlets within each of the four metropolitan boroughs. I have chosen a selection of follies, monuments and curiosities but there are many more I have been unable to include for space reasons.

An Edwardian postcard of the Mansion House, Doncaster. Officially opened on 15 April 1749, the Mansion House is one of only three such mayoral residences in England, the others being at York and the City of London. (*Brian Elliott collection*)

Taken as a whole, Yorkshire has a greater concentration of fine country houses than anywhere in the United Kingdom. South Yorkshire is blessed with many of its own – large country mansions of palatial proportions and more modest country houses or ancient manor houses of superb quality with important historical associations. Those I have selected represent barely the tip of the iceberg. There are so many. Sadly, several disappeared from the landscape during the twentieth century, but there are many beautiful houses still standing, which are all too often ignored. It would be a very thick volume indeed if I had included them all. Churches and chapels are in abundance, but again owing to space reasons I have chosen only a small selection of my favourites. There are a few photographs of some of South Yorkshire's industries, shops, public houses, inns and hotels. For all its omissions, I hope that the book succeeds in capturing some of the essence of South Yorkshire.

I have made every effort to research each image to establish exactly who or what appears in it. I apologise unreservedly for any errors or omissions.

Geoffrey Howse
January 2007

1

Around & About South Yorkshire

The Post Office, Langsett Road, Oughtibridge, early twentieth century. The post office building has a date-stone of 1827. *(Chris Sharp of Old Barnsley)*

Askern is situated about 7 miles north of Doncaster on the main A19 road. The medicinal properties of the mineral water to be found there were first recognised in the eighteenth century. Six boathouses and the Hydro Hotel were built. This E.L. Scrivens postcard shows the Manor Sulphur Baths, Askern Spa. Known locally as the Manor Baths, they comprised a central bath area with promenade rooms in the wings. Boating on the lake was very popular. These boats could hold up to twenty people.
(*Chris Sharp of Old Barnsley*)

By the mid-nineteenth century Askern had become a very fashionable spa town, with recreational facilities at numerous establishments to attract visitors. With the discovery of coal and the introduction of heavy industry in 1911, Askern's popularity as a spa declined. This Edwardian view shows Station Road. The Swan Hotel can be seen at the top of the Market Place.
(*Chris Sharp of Old Barnsley*)

A late Victorian view of Askern High Street. The Crown Hotel can be seen on the left. The lake, at that time a popular tourist attraction, lies immediately behind the buildings on the right.
(*Chris Sharp of Old Barnsley*)

Barnborough, *c.* 1910.
Many seventeenth- and
eighteenth-century buildings
still survive in the older parts
of the village. The village
church, St Peter's, was partly
built in the twelfth century
but most of the remainder is
Decorated and Perpendicular.
(Barry Crabtree collection)

The wooden canal swing-bridge at Barnby Dun, early twentieth century. A canal cut, fed by the River
Don, left the river at Long Sandall. Bridges carrying minor roads and cart tracks were required to span
the canal at several points. One such bridge is shown here. The tower of the Church of St Peter and
St Paul can be seen behind the trees. The church was recorded in the Domesday Book. With the
exception of the Perpendicular tower and carved font, the church is almost completely Decorated. The
chancel was partly rebuilt in 1860, but it retains a medieval sedilia and piscina. In the church is a
memorial to Roger Portington, who supported the Royalist cause during the Civil War. The inscription
reads: 'Approach boldly reader whosoever thou art if a follower of the king; if not, away immediately lest
unknowingly thy wicked foot should touch those pious ashes, for Roger Portington's ashes can ill bear a
rebel's foot – a man who was of an ancient and honourable stock and who suffered imprisonment,
rapine, etc – broken down by old age only, not in spirit – here he lies, with Jane, his wife, waiting for the
last trumpet's call.' *(Chris Sharp of Old Barnsley)*

Following two important meetings held in 1858 at the Old White Bear Inn in Barnsley's Shambles Street (on the site now occupied by Barnsley Central Library), the South Yorkshire Miners' Association was formed. As the movement grew, its ever-expanding facilities required commodious office accommodation. The miners' offices, seen here in this postcard postmarked 10 March 1913, were built at a cost of £8,000 and opened in 1874, at the junction of Huddersfield Road with Old Mill Lane and Victoria Road, Barnsley. The Mence Obelisk dominating the foreground was erected in 1819 as a guidepost by William Cooke Mence (son of the Revd John Mence MA, Curate of Barnsley), a lawyer who occupied several important positions in the town. The obelisk was taken down in 1931, amid claims that its position at a busy junction was causing traffic congestion. During Arthur Scargill's tenure as President of the Yorkshire Miners' Union, the headquarters was popularly known as King Arthur's Court or, more commonly, Camelot. *(Author's collection)*

Market Hill, Barnsley, from an early twentieth-century postcard. *(Author's collection)*

May Day Green,
Barnsley, *c*. 1910.
(Author's collection)

Bawtry was established
as a new town towards
the end of the twelfth
century. This early
Scrivens postcard
shows the Old Butter
Cross and High Street,
before the First World
War. *(Chris Sharp of
Old Barnsley)*

Birdwell Common, at
the junction of The
Walk with Sheffield
Road, early twentieth
century. *(Chris Sharp of
Old Barnsley)*

An Edwardian postcard of the junction of Barnsley Road and Wentworth Road, Blacker Hill. The Royal Albert Hotel, the only public house to remain open in Blacker Hill today, is on the left. The Mission Hall, which served as the village community centre and stood adjacent to Blacker Hill chapel, can be seen in the centre background. *(Doreen Armitage)*

An early twentieth-century view of Wentworth Road, Blacker Hill, facing in the opposite direction to the view above. Blacker Hill post office is in the left foreground, the Blacksmith's Arms is next to it and a little further down the street is the Travellers. Across the road is the Blacker Hill Working Men's Club. *(Chris Sharp of Old Barnsley)*

Brodsworth is an estate village 5 miles north-west of Doncaster. The parish of Brodsworth, which consisted of Pickburn and Old Scawsby, was mentioned in the Domesday Book. A church was erected there in the reign of Edward the Confessor, possibly by the Saxon lord Elsi, who owned extensive lands in the area. This view shows cottages in the early twentieth century, at a spot where routes converge for Pickburn, Doncaster and Hooton Pagnell. *(Chris Sharp of Old Barnsley)*

An early twentieth-century view of cottages in the Butt Lane/Hooton Road part of Brodsworth. *(Chris Sharp of Old Barnsley)*

A view of Broomhill from Manchester Road, 1902. *(Doreen Howse collection)*

Rotherham Road, Catcliffe, beyond which is the end of Whitehill Lane, *c.* 1905. On the right are the railings of the County Primary and Infants' School. Situated about 4 miles south of Rotherham, in a semi-rural location, Catcliffe lies alongside the River Rother. A striking feature of Catcliffe is its glass-blowing kiln, one of two built in 1740 by William Fenny. The glassworks operated until 1884, and reopened briefly in 1901 before falling into a ruinous condition. The surviving cone was threatened with demolition in the 1960s. Restored, it is now a protected monument and is one of only five such kilns in the British Isles. *(Chris Sharp of Old Barnsley)*

An early twentieth-century view of the picturesque village of Cawthorne. *(Brian Elliott collection)*

White Lane, Chapeltown, early twentieth century. Little evidence of a settlement here exists before the twelfth century. There are some fine country residences with ancient origins in the immediate area, including Howsley Hall and Cowley Manor. More evidence survives of a settlement of a considerable size after the introduction of Chapeltown Furnace to this highly wooded area, around 1600. The woods provided charcoal for the furnace. It was after Mr Newton and Mr Chambers founded Thorncliffe Ironworks in 1793, on land leased from Earl Fitzwilliam, that Chapeltown began to develop into a larger community. The Station Inn can be seen on the left. *(Author's collection)*

A Leyland Atlantean, Yorkshire Traction double-decker passing the Izal Factory in Chapeltown, 1965. *(Keith Atack)*

An early twentieth-century view of Conisborough, seen from Clifton Hill. Conisborough Castle is hidden behind the trees to the right of St Peter's Church, whose tower can be seen in the centre skyline. St Peter's Church is South Yorkshire's oldest surviving building, the original church being built in AD 650–700. Part of the Saxon structure survives in the nave but most of the church is Norman with some Perpendicular additions. *(Chris Sharp of Old Barnsley)*

Opposite, top: Station Road, Conisborough, 1920s postcard. *(Chris Sharp of Old Barnsley)*

Opposite, bottom: Photographed from the junction with Duncan Road, this postcard shows Crookes in about 1920. *(Doreen Howse collection)*

A pre-1912 view of Clock Corner, French Gate, Doncaster, seen from St Sepulchre Gate. The present building with the clock tower replaced another, which also had a clock. The building seen here was erected in 1895 to the design of architect J.G. Walker (1850–1930), who was born in the old building at Clock Corner. He designed this building as his own offices. The building on the right with the large dome is the Midland Bank, designed by W.H. Brierley (1862–1926) in the English Baroque style. *(Chris Sharp of Old Barnsley)*

Below: An early Scrivens postcard looking across Clock Corner from French Gate, into High Street, Doncaster. *(Chris Sharp of Old Barnsley)*

Station Road, Doncaster, during the Edwardian period. On the left corner is the Doncaster Mutual Co-operative Society; in the centre is the Glyn Commercial Hotel, named after the Revd Edward Carr Glyn, Vicar of St George's and a principal promoter of the temperance movement in Doncaster. The Grand Theatre (opened 1899), which pre-dates Station Road, can be seen at the end of the road. Station Road opened on 11 August 1902 and was the terminus for several tram routes. *(Chris Sharp of Old Barnsley)*

A postcard of Station Road and St Sepulchre Gate, Doncaster, *c.* 1920. *(Chris Sharp of Old Barnsley)*

The village of Dore in the early twentieth century; one of the loveliest villages in the Sheffield area and a highly desirable place to live. *(Chris Sharp of Old Barnsley)*

Victoria Road, Edlington, *c.* 1915. The York Hotel, built in 1913, can be seen at the bottom of the street. Its front faces onto Edlington Lane. *(Chris Sharp of Old Barnsley)*

Howse's Corner, Elsecar, seen from Forge Lane, *c.* 1895. The name has been used since about that time, after William and Martha Howse opened a confectionery, a grocery and general store. Howse's shop (left foreground) is at 1 Wentworth Road, situated opposite the Market Hotel at the junction of Fitzwilliam Street and Wentworth Road. Wath Road goes off to the right and Elsecar Market Hall, built by the 6th Earl Fitzwilliam and opened on Christmas Eve 1870, can be seen in the right-hand foreground. *(Author's collection)*

An Edwardian view of St Helen's Street, Elsecar. St Helen's Street and the Roman Catholic church built there in 1866 and dedicated to St Helen were named after the mother of the Roman Emperor Constantine. The church was relocated to West Street, Hoyland, after the Midland Railway Company bought the site in the 1890s. *(Chris Sharp of Old Barnsley)*

An early twentieth-century view of Occupation Road, Harley, a small village sandwiched between Tankersley Park and the larger estate village of Wentworth. *(Chris Sharp of Old Barnsley)*

Withens Avenue, Hillsborough, *c.* 1910. *(Chris Sharp of Old Barnsley)*

The Old Butter Cross, Hooton Pagnell, early twentieth century. The cross, thought to date from 1253, stands in a commanding position with extensive views over the surrounding countryside. The Pound, a small walled enclosure where cattle that had strayed were impounded, is immediately behind the cross (out of sight). *(Chris Sharp of Old Barnsley)*

The Hostel, Hooton Pagnell, shortly after it was built in 1903. The mock-Tudor building was originally a theological college for St Chad's. St Chad's moved to Durham before the First World War to become part of the university. During the war the Hostel was used as a convalescent home. *(Chris Sharp of Old Barnsley)*

One of Lichie Walker's postcards of King Street and High Street, Hoyland, *c.* 1925. Lichie Walker's newsagents and stationery shop can be seen on the right, at 8 King Street. Further up on the right, in High Street, is the John Knowles Memorial Church, a church of the Free Church of England, whose foundation stones were laid in September 1911. On the left can be seen the clock tower of Hoyland Town Hall. The clock was known as 'Old Martha' after its benefactor Martha Knowles, a prominent local businesswoman. (*Author's collection*)

HOOTON PAGNELL.

CHURCH.

THE HALL.

HOOTON PAGNELL.

LYCH GATE.

THE HOSTEL.

Greetings from Jump.

Main Street, Mexborough, during the late Victorian period. Mexborough was described in the Domesday Book as Mechesburgh (a meeting place or coming together). Situated on the north bank of the River Don, it is 6 miles west of Doncaster. In 1811 it had a population of 403 but during the nineteenth century it grew to be a medium-sized town. In 1877 the *South Yorkshire Times* was established there. Still flourishing, it is sold over a wide area. The television presenter and journalist Michael Parkinson began his career in Mexborough. *(Chris Sharp of Old Barnsley)*

Opposite, top: A composite postcard of Hooton Pagnell. Featured are the substantially Norman All Saints' Church, enlarged during the twelfth and thirteenth centuries and restored by John Loughborough Pearson in 1875; the Lych Gate; the Hall, dating from the fourteenth century, and home to the Warde-Norbury family; the Hostel; and a village scene. *(Chris Sharp of Old Barnsley)*

Opposite, bottom: A composite view of Jump and district, early 1900s. In the centre is St George's Church. Hemingfield Road. Also featured are the impressive entrance to Jump Cemetery, Wombwell Wood and Wombwell railway station. *(Keith Hopkinson collection)*

An early twentieth-century postcard of Church Street, Oughtibridge. A relatively plain but perfectly functional village, then and now, Oughtibridge is greatly enhanced by the spectacular countryside that surrounds it. *(Chris Sharp of Old Barnsley)*

An engraving of the old town of Rotherham. The medieval Town Hall dominates the left background. *(Brian Elliott collection)*

A view down Fargate towards High Street, Sheffield, *c.* 1902. *(Doreen Howse collection)*

Fitzalan Square, Sheffield, 1900. Situated at the bottom of High Street at its junction with Commercial Street and Haymarket, the square's name derives from a branch of the Howard family, Howard being the family name of the dukes of Norfolk. This open space was created in 1881 on the site of buildings that had been demolished in Market Street. The Fitzalan Market Hall can be seen across the square with Haymarket to its right. *(Author's collection)*

A late 1960s postcard showing Goodwin Fountain and, behind it, Wilson Peck, the popular Sheffield music store, situated at the corner of Leopold Street and Barker's Pool. *(Author's collection)*

Castle Market, on a postcard franked 22 June 1966. The market, which opened in 1959, replaced the Norfolk Market Hall. The few fragments that remain of the once extensive Sheffield Castle lie beneath the market complex. *(Author's collection)*

This composite Scrivens postcard of Sprotborough probably dates from just after the First World War, as Sprotborough Hall (bottom left) was demolished in 1926. Other views are of St Mary's Church, the mill, which ceased production in 1933 and was later demolished, Sprotborough Bridge, and the locks. *(Chris Sharp of Old Barnsley)*

An early twentieth-century view of Main Street, Sprotborough, showing estate cottages belonging to the Copley family, owners of the Sprotborough Hall Estate. *(Chris Sharp of Old Barnsley)*

Market Place, Thorne, from an early Scrivens postcard. Thorne became a settlement in Anglo-Saxon times. This attractive market town situated 11 miles north of Doncaster had its first market charter granted in 1658. It still has a busy market on Tuesdays, Fridays and Saturdays. *(Chris Sharp of Old Barnsley)*

A Scrivens postcard of Church Street, Thorne, produced during the late Edwardian period. The parish church of St Nicholas can be seen at the end of the narrow street. This Early English church has a Decorated tower. The belfry, clerestory, chapels and its two-storeyed porch are Perpendicular. *(Chris Sharp of Old Barnsley)*

Another Edwardian Scrivens postcard of Finkle Street, Thorne. *(Chris Sharp of Old Barnsley)*

A Scrivens postcard of the Swing Bridge, Thorne, in operation during the late Edwardian period. *(Chris Sharp of Old Barnsley)*

Castle Gate and the Market Place, Tickhill, *c.* 1930. On the left is the Butter Cross. This market cross, erected by the Revd Christopher Alsderson in about 1777, is situated at the convergence of several major routes. The water pump immediately in front of the Butter Cross commemorates the Diamond Jubilee of Queen Victoria (1897). The attractive town of Tickhill can trace its origins to pre-Roman times. It developed into a settlement of considerable size shortly after 1066, when William the Conqueror rewarded one of his Norman supporters with the gift of several manors in the north of England, one of which included the lands around Tickhill. *(Chris Sharp of Old Barnsley)*

A 1920s Scrivens postcard of Mill Dam, Tickhill, looking towards the tower of St Mary's Church. *(Chris Sharp of Old Barnsley)*

Opposite: Hillfoot Road, Totley, *c.* 1900. The house in the foreground on the right was known as Avalon. The semi-detached Victorian villas on the hillside on the left are called Doris and Vera. *(Chris Sharp of Old Barnsley)*

Below: A view of the hamlet of Upper Hoyland and its surrounding countryside, seen from Hoyland Law Stand. The spire of St Mary's Church, Worsborough, can be seen near the left-hand skyline. Upper Hoyland Hall can be seen in the centre of the image. *(Courtesy of Ivy Conway)*

Wadsley lies on the north-western edge of Sheffield on one of the seven hills on which the city was built. Some of the substantial late Victorian villas in Wadsley Lane are seen here in the early Edwardian period. *(Chris Sharp of Old Barnsley)*

An early twentieth-century view of Low Road West, Warmsworth. Situated 3 miles west of Doncaster, Warmsworth is an ancient village, recorded in the Domesday Book. Until 1750 it was mainly a farming community. However, after the potential for quarrying high-quality magnesium limestone was realised, many established and new residents became engaged in this new form of work. *(Chris Sharp of Old Barnsley)*

Paradise Square, Wentworth, *c.* 1910. Known by this name from about 1900, the buildings seen here were once a farm. The farmhouse is at the top left of the photograph, although the original farmhouse is believed to have been part of one of the adjacent buildings. This attractive group of buildings was converted into cottages during the eighteenth century. *(Sandra Hague collection)*

A Lichie Walker postcard of Main Street, Wentworth, 1920s. *(Walkers Newsagents collection)*

Activity in Station Road, Woodhouse, as children go home from school, *c.* 1910. *(Chris Sharp of Old Barnsley)*

The Big Tree Hotel, Chesterfield Road, Woodseats, *c.* 1900. This eighteenth-century inn was formerly called the Masons Arms. A large horse chestnut tree stands in the forecourt, from which the public house takes its name. *(Sheffield Central Library)*

2

Parks, Woods, Gardens & Beauty Spots

Corinthian columns in Barnsley's Locke Park. St Edward's Church, Kingstone, can be seen in the centre background. Locke Park was laid out on land donated to the town in 1861 by the widow of the engineer Joseph Locke, who spent his formative years in Barnsley. The park opened on 10 June 1862. *(Author's collection))*

The entrance gates and lodge at Locke Park, Barnsley, early 1900s. *(Author's collection)*

The fountain, Locke Park, Barnsley, completed in 1879, is seen here in the early 1900s. *(Author's collection)*

Townsend Park, Barnsley, from a 1920s postcard. *(Author's collection)*

Early twentieth-century postcard of Wilthorpe Park, Barnsley. *(Author's collection)*

An early twentieth-century Valentine's postcard of Beauchief Gardens. *(Author's collection)*

Crookes Valley Park and Dam, Crookesmoor, from a postcard franked 9 June 1909. *(Author's collection)*

A large reservoir had existed at Elsecar since the closing years of the eighteenth century, when it was built to feed the Elsecar branch of the Dearne and Dove Canal. In about 1910 a Sheffield barber called Herbert Parkin opened a shop in the area of Elsecar known as Stubbin. An accomplished amateur photographer, he spent his spare time photographing local subjects. He took some views of Elsecar Reservoir and the surrounding area and sent them to the *Sheffield Star*, which published them with the caption 'Elsecar-by-the-Sea'. This is a 1920s Lichie Walker postcard of 'The Beach, Elsecar'. *(Walkers Newsagents collection)*

Herbert Parkin's photographs struck the right note with the people of Sheffield, and, as Elsecar could easily be reached by rail, there began an exodus to the village to escape the grime of the city – a special treat for children who rarely saw the countryside. Elsecar proved so popular an attraction that the idea of creating a public park was born. Hoyland UDC built a refreshment room and an artificial beach was created and boats sailed on the reservoir, referred to by some during that period as 'the lake' and by others as Elsecar Lido. Such was the popularity of Elsecar-by-the-Sea that a full range of postcards was produced. This one is entitled 'The Landing Stage, Elsecar Harbour'. *(Margaret Gaddass collection)*

The park was divided into two main areas. The top park (right) was next to the reservoir, with its boating facilities and joy rides; the bottom park (above, 1950s) was laid out with flowerbeds and also contained a paddling pool. The soubriquet Elsecar-by-the-Sea lasted for decades. Always attractive, Elsecar Park has recently undergone a major restoration programme. *(George Hardy collection)*

Below: An early postcard of 'The Beach, Elsecar-by-the-Sea'. The hamlet of Skiers Hall can be seen on the centre skyline. *(George Hardy collection)*

The River Porter has its source in the moors above Sheffield and flows eastwards about 14 miles into the heart of the city. Its valley is a green corridor in which was created Bingham Park and, on a site beside Endcliffe Woods and on the opposite side of Rustlings Road to Bingham Park, Endcliffe Park, during the latter half of the nineteenth century. This 1890s postcard shows Endcliffe Park and the entrance to Endcliffe Woods. *(Author's collection)*

A postcard, franked 29 June 1904, of the dam, Endcliffe Woods. *(Author's collection)*

A postcard, franked 24 August 1907, with the inscription: 'The Duck Pond, Firth Park'. The 36-acre park, designed by Flockton and Abbot in 1874, was donated to the people of Sheffield by Mark Firth in 1875 and officially opened by HRH the Prince of Wales later that year. The 'Duck Pond' has also been used for sailing toy boats and as a paddling pool. The clock tower and refreshment room can be seen in the centre background. *(Author's collection)*

A pre-First World War view of the boating lake at Forge Dam, Fulwood. The boathouse can be seen on the right. *(Author's collection)*

An early twentieth-century view of the lake, Hillsborough Park. (*Author's collection*)

An early Kromo series postcard of the Loxley Valley. (*Author's collection*)

The Boating Lake, Millhouses Park, from a postcard franked 25 August 1959. (*Author's collection*)

A postcard, franked 6 September 1920, of Boston Park, Rotherham. (*Author's collection*)

The Botanical Gardens, Sheffield, were laid out on a 19-acre site to the west of the city centre, to the designs of Robert Marnock. This early twentieth-century postcard features the three pavilions designed by Sir Joseph Paxton (1801–65) in 1837. *(Author's collection)*

Graves Park, covering some 200 acres on the southern outskirts of the city, is Sheffield's largest park. The parkland had existed for centuries and was saved from development by Alderman J.G. Graves, a principal benefactor in Sheffield. He bought the land in stages between 1926 and 1936, and donated the park to the people of Sheffield to be kept as parkland in perpetuity. This postcard, franked 10 July 1962, shows Graves Park's beautifully stocked flowerbeds and manicured lawns. *(Author's collection)*

An early Edwardian postcard showing the entrance gates of Norfolk Park, Sheffield. Norfolk Park was one of the first public parks in the country, opened in 1848 on land belonging to the Duke of Norfolk. It incorporates a main circular carriageway with two avenues, planted with lime trees and turkey oaks. In 1910 the Duke of Norfolk gave the park to the City of Sheffield. *(Author's collection)*

The Mappin Art Gallery, Weston Park, in a Valentine's postcard from about 1900. The gallery was built at a cost of £15,000 between 1886 and 1888, to the designs of architects Flockton and Gibbs. It has a long colonnaded front in the Ionic order and was founded under the terms of the will of John Newton Mappin, a wealthy cutlery manufacturer, who bequeathed 153 paintings. His nephew, Sir Frederick Mappin, presented a further forty-eight, and other bequests followed. *(Author's collection)*

The 'Strafford Oak', Tankersley Park, where local tradition has it Lord Strafford was 'arrested', seen here in about 1930. In 1640 Tankersley Park had become part of the extensive estate belonging to Thomas Wentworth, 1st Earl of Strafford (1593–1641). When the 'Long Parliament' met on 3 November 1640 King Charles I needed Strafford's counsel and sent for him. Strafford was His Majesty's loyal supporter, chief minister and friend. Traditionally it is said that when the King's men arrived at Wentworth Woodhouse they were sent to Tankersley Park, where they found Lord Strafford beneath the oak tree shown here. Strafford was not in fact arrested but merely asked to accompany the party back to London at the King's request. Yet even on Ordnance Survey maps the site of the tree is marked 'The Oak Tree in which it is said Lord Strafford was arrested', which added spice to the legend. Lord Strafford left Wentworth Woodhouse for London on 6 November with, in his own words, 'more dangers beset, I believe, than ever a man went out of Yorkshire'. He was impeached later that month and committed to the Tower of London on 25 November. At his trial in Westminster Hall in January 1641 Strafford defended himself with great skill and could not be found guilty of any of the charges his enemies had brought against him. In order to get rid of this most gifted English statesman they found him guilty by an Act of Parliament, the Act of Attainder. He was beheaded on Tower Hill by Richard Brandon on 12 May 1641. (*Author's collection*)

An early postcard of Wharncliffe Crags, situated north-west of Sheffield. Before road and rail transport made distant attractions more accessible, Wharncliffe Crags was a popular place to visit for people from all over South Yorkshire, particularly at Easter and Whitsuntide, when it was not unusual for there to be hundreds of visitors. (*Author's collection*)

Whitely Wood and the River Porter, 1910. (*Author's collection*)

An early twentieth-century composite postcard showing the various delights to be seen at Wyming Brook, situated to the east of the city. (*Author's collection*)

A 1920s postcard of Hollow Meadows Dams, Wyming Brook. The wooded slopes of Wyming Brook open out to views of the Hollow Meadows Dams in the Rivelin Valley. (*Author's collection*)

3
South Yorkshire's Industries

Clifford Willoughby (left) and Ernest Brasher, cold rolling strip steel at J.J. Habershon, Holmes Mills, Rotherham, in 1950. *(Clifford & Margaret Willoughby)*

The 7th Earl Fitzwilliam and his wife, Countess Maud, outside Wentworth Woodhouse, with one of their Simplex motor cars, registration number LK 4496. Manufactured in Sheffield, the Simplex was designed in the stable block at Wentworth Woodhouse. In 1906 Lord Fitzwilliam offered a plot of his land in Sheffield to the Brotherhood-Crocker Car Company, to build a motor car manufacturing plant. Opened in 1908, it was known as The Simplex Motor Works Ltd. Lord Fitzwilliam was the major shareholder. Various models were made there until 1925. The last, a 50hp model, was built for the Earl's private use. Bearing the number plate PE 1717, it spent some time at Wentworth before being taken to Ireland to the Fitzwilliam's Coollattin Estate. Sold in the 1960s, the car now forms part of the collection at Kelham Island Museum in Sheffield. (*Author's collection*)

Opposite, top: Doncaster had one motor manufacturer, the Cheswold, named after a river flowing through the town. More than a hundred Cheswold cars were made in the Doncaster works of E.W. Jackson & Son Ltd between 1910 and 1914. The engine was a 4-cylinder 15.9hp, with a four-speed 'crash' gearbox. Production ceased at the beginning of the First World War, and the marque was never revived. (*Barry Crabtree collection*)

Opposite, bottom: A repair shop at the Great Northern Railway headquarters, Doncaster, 1912. GNR established the headquarters of their engine and coach-building plant here in 1853. Over 6,000 hands were employed in building locomotives and carriages at that time. The site covered 80 acres, with an additional 55 acres of sidings. (*Barry Crabtree collection*)

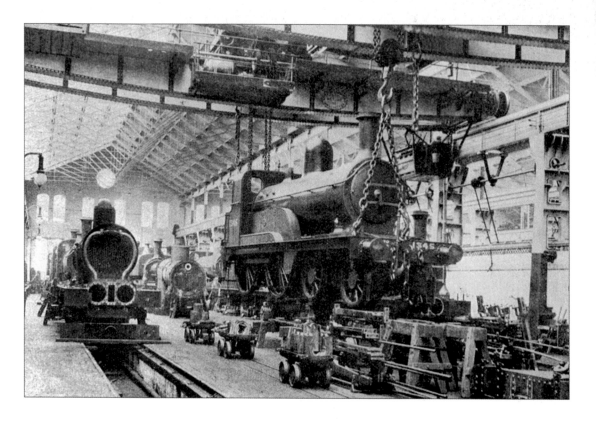

Elsecar's celebrated Newcomen-type engine, situated in the area of Elsecar known as Distillery Side or, in local parlance, 'Stillery Side'. It was constructed in 1795 on a site adjacent to Earl Fitzwilliam's Elsecar New Colliery, which was sunk in the same year. This is the only engine of its type in the world, which remains on its original site. Considered Elsecar's major asset, it is the most important surviving artefact of South Yorkshire's early industrial expansion. In 1927 Henry Ford paid a secret visit to Elsecar, during a tour of industrial areas throughout the country. His intention was to take exhibits back to the Ford Museum in Detroit. He expressed a strong interest in the engine at Elsecar. However, someone politely pointed out to Mr Ford that the engine was not for sale at any price. *(Author's collection)*

Already well established for centuries as the most important centre for cutlery production, from the late seventeenth century onwards Sheffield became renowned for its production of high-quality steels. The Industrial Revolution saw a rapid increase in population from 10,121 in 1736 to 31,314 in 1801. In 1970, 45,000 people were working in the steel and cutlery industries in Sheffield. By the mid-1980s the number had fallen to 12,000 and by 2001 there were fewer than 8,000 steel and cutlery workers. Numbers continue to decline. Modern production methods mean that one man can now accomplish a job that once required ten. This image, from about 1900, shows the Clyde Steelworks of Samuel Osborn and Co. Ltd on the banks of the River Don, a major employer of the time The steelworks were situated between the Wicker and the River Don. Sheffield's Royal Victoria Hotel can be seen on the right. *(David J. Richardson collection)*

Workers at Samuel Staniforth's central cutlery works, Carver Street, Sheffield, in 1900. This view shows the forging shop, where cutlery blanks were made. The cutlery works opened in 1864 and operated until 1982. *(Doreen Howse collection)*

An aerial view of Hoyland Brick Co. Ltd,
1959. The Barnsley (Courthouse
station) to Sheffield (Great Central)
railway line can be seen, and beyond it
the single Derby line to Rockingham and
Wharncliffe Silkstone Collieries.
(David Doughty collection)

Gimlet making in Ecclesfield. Mr John
Thomas Ridge retired aged 90; his
retirement and the closure of his smithy
in Ecclesfield, in 1969, severed a link
with the metal-working industries of the
village which had existed for over 800
years. *(Photographed by Cyril Slinn)*

Ironmasters George Newton and Thomas Chambers approached the 4th Earl Fitzwilliam in 1793 regarding leasing a site in the Blackburn Brook valley for an ironworks. The firm of Newton Chambers became a major employer at their Thorncliffe works, and remained so for more than 150 years. The story of Izal, which became a household name, began in 1885, in Chapeltown, on the Thorncliffe site, when the analytical chemist, J.H. Worrall, came to Thorncliffe to undertake research on the gas from the beehive ovens. He turned his attention to the liquid product of the gas and then to the oil which was also produced. As a result he developed a germicidal oil which proved effective against sheep scab. The product was initially marketed as a sheep dip under the name Noxona and exported to New Zealand under the name Acaricide. It was marketed as Thorncliffe Patent Disinfectant before finally being given the name Izal, registered in 1893. There is a popularly held belief that the name is an anagram of its discoverer's favourite sister, Liza. This is an aerial view of Thorncliffe Chemical Works from about 1930. *(Keith Atack collection)*

Below: Advertisements which appeared in *The Illustrated London News* in 1893 and 1906. *(Author's collection)*

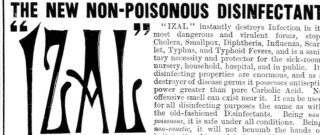

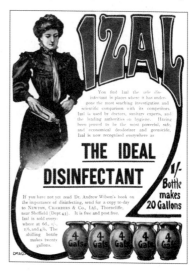

Earthenware pottery had been made on the Swinton site (later the Rockingham Works) since 1745, when Edward Butler rented the land on which the property was built from the Earl of Malton (who became the 1st Marquess of Rockingham the following year). Several changes in ownership followed. Various members of the Brameld family became associated with the firm and in 1806 William Brameld and his son John took over the pottery works and began manufacturing wares under their own name. They appealed to the 4th Earl Fitzwilliam (who in 1782 had inherited the vast estates of his uncle, Charles, 2nd Marquess of Rockingham) for financial assistance to help run the works. The Earl obliged and the Brameld business flourished; by the time John Brameld died in 1819 it had a workforce of some 300. Various family members continued to run the works and John's sons George and John travelled extensively as salesmen. The Bramelds produced wares of the highest quality and the firm had many foreign clients. Despite a substantial market for their products, the Bramelds were notoriously bad businessmen. In the aftermath of the Napoleonic Wars they enthusiastically produced their wares but neglected to chase the money owed to them. The devaluing of Russian currency caused them severe financial problems, compounded by large debts built up through their other foreign dealings. Such was their lack of business acumen that they often sold their high-quality items at a loss. By 1826 the Bramelds were facing bankruptcy. This nineteenth-century engraving shows the Rockingham Works at Swinton. (*Author's collection*)

Once again, Earl Fitzwilliam was asked for assistance to bail out the Bramelds. His Lordship's appreciation of the fine quality of the goods produced persuaded him to help, but he imposed conditions: sales were to be restricted to the home market, and the pottery should henceforward be known as the Rockingham Works. From 1826, when the Bramelds began to produce porcelain (china), a griffin became part of their trademark and was featured on all wares produced there. The griffin, long associated with the owners of Wentworth Woodhouse, appeared in red on Rockingham ware until 1830, when it was changed to puce. The Bramelds produced a magnificent 200-piece dinner service for William IV, after which the words 'Manufacturer to the King' appeared below the familiar trademark. Despite the diversity, quality and popularity of their wares, the Bramelds remained poor businessmen, a failing that led to their downfall. Lord Fitzwilliam died in 1833. His son, the 5th Earl, continued to give occasional assistance to the Rockingham Works, but over time he lost patience with their business failures and decided that the works should be closed. A large auction of Rockingham pottery took place in May 1842 and one month later the Rockingham Works was advertised to let. Although various types of pottery were produced at the works for several years afterwards, Rockingham pottery ceased to be manufactured in 1842. The Waterloo Kiln, the only remaining kiln on the Rockingham Works site, is seen in this 1990s view from across Pottery Pond; to the left of the kiln is Strawberry Cottage. With the exception of one of the twin gatehouses, the kiln and Strawberry Cottage, adapted to form a dwelling from part of the buildings seen in the previous image, are all that remains of the once substantial Rockingham Works. *(George Hardy collection)*

The premises of the famous Sheffield company Henderson's, situated on the corner of Leavygreave Road and Upper Hanover Street, 1998. Henry Henderson opened his business in Broad Lane in the closing years of the nineteenth century. The firm has been producing its celebrated Henderson's Relish within a half-mile radius of the original factory ever since. Relish of all kinds was very popular during the late Victorian period, particularly in Yorkshire. Most firms that produced it have long since disappeared, or been incorporated into other companies, their products being made to original recipes far away from where they were first conceived. In its early days Henderson's Relish developed a reputation for its medicinal properties. The bottle in which the relish is sold has hardly changed over the years, only the size has varied. The clear bottles, with their long, thin necks and bright orange labels, filled with a dark aromatic liquid, once had red or orange tops. The black caps now incorporate handy shakers. The very first bottles would have cork stoppers sealed with wax. Three-quarters of a million bottles are sold each year in Yorkshire alone. Henry Henderson could never have imagined that his relish would one day cross the Atlantic in the baggage of some of Sheffield's most famous sons. Pop stars and other celebrities from Sheffield have openly admitted that a bottle of Henderson's Relish goes with them on their travels. *(Sheffield Central Library)*

Coal mining was an important industry in South Yorkshire for hundreds of years. There are reminders of this once prolific industry throughout the area. This is Cortonwood Colliery, whose threatened closure brought it to the forefront of the 1984–5 miners' strike. This photograph was taken a few days after the mine finally closed in May 1986. In the foreground is former Wharncliffe Silkstone miner Arthur K. Clayton (1901–2002), a noted local historian whose meticulous research uncovered a wealth of hitherto unknown facts about South Yorkshire's history. His findings have proved invaluable to other historians, myself included. *(Brian Elliott collection)*

4

Churches & Ecclesiastical Buildings

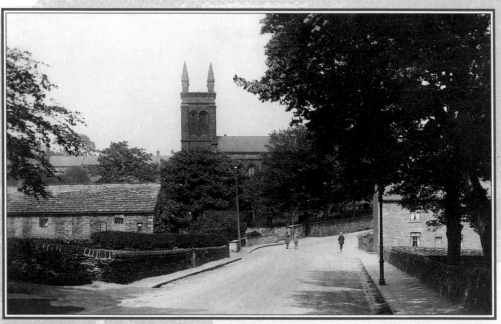

St John's Church, Dodworth, built by public subscription at a cost of £2,518 and consecrated by the Bishop of Ripon in 1848. *(Brian Elliott collection)*

An early twentieth-century postcard of St Laurence's Church, Adwick Le Street. This ancient church has some Norman work. The Elizabethan Washington tomb of 1579 is of particular interest. James Washington, who lived at Adwick Hall (long since demolished), is dressed in armour. His coat of arms bears three stars and stripes, giving rise to a connection with George Washington – which is why Adwick Le Street receives many American visitors. There are several monuments to members of the Fitzwilliam family, landowners on a large scale throughout South Yorkshire and beyond since the reign of William the Conqueror. The church also has some fine stained glass by J.E. Nuttgens, depicting stories of St Francis. In this image the Foresters Arms can be seen in the distance. Adwick Le Street is situated near to the Roman road that ran from Doncaster to Castleford. The site of an ancient castle and that of a moated manor house are nearby. (Chris Sharp of Old Barnsley)

St Mary's Church, Barnsley. This ancient chapel of ease fell within the parish of Silkstone. Largely rebuilt in 1820–1 by Thomas Rickman in the style of the early fourteenth century, it has a Perpendicular tower. (Author's collection)

St George's Church, Barnsley, *c.* 1910. Known as a 'Waterloo church', St George's was one of several churches built at the expense of a grateful government to commemorate the defeat of Napoleon's forces by the Duke of Wellington and his allies in 1815. It was built in 1821 to the design of Thomas Rickman and enlarged several times. Rickman used iron in its construction, the gradual deterioration of which resulted in severe structural damage and the church's abandonment. Some of St George's features were salvaged and incorporated into a new building.
(Author's collection)

The 'Light of the World' window, rescued from the demolished St George's Church, Barnsley, and incorporated in the new church in 1987. The window is based on a painting by the Pre-Raphaelite artist William Holman Hunt.
(Brian Elliott collection)

St Thomas Becket's Church, Beauchief. This image shows part of the west end of Beauchief Abbey, founded in about 1175 and incorporated into the church here. Although it once stood in splendid isolation Beauchief Abbey has been hemmed in by Sheffield's sprawling suburbs. Fortunately a golf course preserves some of the open landscape that still surrounds this semi-ruin. *(Author's collection)*

Situated on a hill above Stocksbridge, the village of Bolsterstone stands 984ft above sea level and is surrounded by spectacular scenery. St Mary's Church, seen here in about 1910, is one of a succession of churches in Bolsterstone and was built between 1872 and 1879 at a cost of £7,200. A list of incumbents is displayed in the church dating from 1412 to the present. The buildings to the left of the church form part of the Castle Inn. During the mid-twentieth century the Castle Inn was owned by Sam Costa, well known for his radio broadcasts, including *ITMA*. The inn is named after the castle built nearby by the Sheffield family in 1250, of which a few fragments remain. *(Chris Sharp of Old Barnsley)*

St Nicholas's Church, Bradfield, *c.* 1905. This imposing building, situated on a hillside surrounded by countryside, was erected in 1109 by the Lovetot family, who became lords of the manor during the reign of William the Conqueror. The Lovetots also built St Mary's Church, Ecclesfield, to whose enormous parish this church became a chapel of ease until 1868. A square bell tower was added to the Norman structure in the fourteenth century, and soon afterwards the church was enlarged and remodelled in the Gothic Perpendicular style. To the north of the main gates and visible to the right of this postcard image can be seen a watch house. This was built in 1831 to safeguard newly buried bodies from being snatched by resurrectionists to be anatomised in Sheffield's rapidly expanding medical schools. *(Chris Sharp of Old Barnsley)*

Bullhouse Chapel, Bullhouse, near Penistone. Following the Restoration in 1660, Elkanah Rich of Bullhouse Hall registered his home as a meeting place for Protestant dissenters. He later built a chapel in his grounds. Seen here in 1997, and situated in Bullhouse Lane, 2 miles west of Thurlstone, and generally known as the Dissenters' Chapel, Bullhouse Independent Chapel was completed in 1692. The interior is panelled in oak and there is an extremely fine pulpit dating from the chapel's foundation. *(Brian Elliott collection)*

John Jarratt paid the building costs for Christ Church, Doncaster. The Mayor of Doncaster, Richard Littlejohn, laid the foundation stone on 9 October 1827 and building continued until 1829. The spire was struck by lightning in 1836, and further damage occurred in 1850 before the chancel was enlarged by Sir Gilbert Scott. There is some Belgian glass by Jean Capronnier in the apse. *(Author's collection)*

Opposite, top: All Saints' Church, Darfield, seen here with a light dusting of snow during the 1980s. Most of the church is fourteenth-century, excepting the upper part of the tower, which is fifteenth-century. There is Jacobean woodwork in the pews, communion rail and font cover. A family pew incorporates early sixteenth-century bench ends. The south aisle has an eighteenth-century painted ceiling. In the churchyard is a monument in the form of an obelisk, now blackened by time, to 189 men and boys who were killed in the Lundhill Colliery disaster of 1859. In the foreground of the image, surrounded by iron railings, is the tomb of Ebenezer Elliott (1787–1849), generally known as the 'Corn Law Rhymer'. Elliott gained a national reputation in the 1830s. He passionately believed in relieving the suffering of ordinary people. His poems set him apart from his contemporary poets and he was regarded by some as a political protagonist who held dangerously radical views. He died aged 68 at Hargate Hill Farm, Great Houghton, on 1 December 1849. *(Brian Elliott collection)*

Opposite, bottom: An early twentieth-century Machan postcard of All Saints' Church, Darton. This wholly Perpendicular church gradually replaced an earlier structure, which was partly rebuilt by the Cluniac monks of Monk Bretton Priory, under the auspices of the prior, Thomas Tykyll, who took care of the chancel while the parishioners rebuilt the nave. The tower is part of the earlier structure. An inscription on a wall plate states that work on the chancel was completed in 1517, when Richard Hunter was vicar there. There is some fine woodwork in the ceilings, communion rail and screens, and fragments of medieval and some early Tudor glass in the north chapel, notably the figure of St Mary Magdalene, depicted full length with a halo. She holds a long tress of her hair, with which she dried Christ's feet after washing them with her tears. *(Author's collection)*

St George's Church, Doncaster, seen here in a 1920s Scrivens postcard, taken from the north bank of the River Don. For centuries the medieval church, built in about 1200, dominated the townscape. A disastrous fire destroyed the old church in 1853. The present church, opened in 1858, was built to a design of Sir Gilbert Scott in magnesium limestone and closely resembles the old building. Cruciform in style, its tower, centrally positioned and rising to 170ft, is the most prominent local landmark. Sir Nikolaus Pevsner considered St George's to be 'the proudest and most cathedral-like' of Sir Gilbert Scott's parish churches. (*Chris Sharp of Old Barnsley*)

Above: St Peter's Church, Edlington, *c.* 1918. This ancient church has Norman stonework in the nave, the lower parts of the tower and the chancel. The upper part of the tower dates from the fifteenth century. The chancel was rebuilt in the thirteenth century. Today St Peter's is redundant and is looked after by the Churches Conservation Trust. The creeper has been removed from the walls and tower and regrettably, like so many others elsewhere, the iron railings were removed from the tombs during the Second World War. *(Chris Sharp of Old Barnsley)*

Holy Trinity Church, Elsecar, *c.* 1950. On Whit Monday 1841 the 5th Earl Fitzwilliam laid the foundation stone of Holy Trinity Church, which was built at his own expense at a cost of £2,500. Constructed in Early English style, with its main axis running from south to north, it took two years to build and opened for worship on Whit Monday, 6 June 1843, having been consecrated by the Archbishop of York. For several years the church remained in the parish of All Saints, Wath-upon-Dearne, until the parish of Elsecar came into existence in 1855. *(Author's collection)*

Above: Sir Edward Rhodes's Chapel, Great Houghton. The Nonconformist Rhodes family lived at Great Houghton Hall, built during the reign of Elizabeth I for Sir Godfrey Rhodes by his father, Francis, of Stavely Woodthorpe in Derbyshire. The family remained in residence until 1789. The hall then had a succession of residents before it became an inn, which was gutted by fire in 1960 and subsequently demolished. In about 1650 Sir Edward Rhodes (whose sister, Elizabeth, had married Thomas Wentworth 1st Earl of Strafford in October 1632) built a chapel in the grounds of the hall. After a succession of dissenting ministers, in 1743 at the Archbishop of York's visitation, the chapel was described as 'united to the church of England'. Today the chapel is dedicated to St Michael and All Hallows. The chapel has crow-stepped gables and curved battlements, and an attractive interior with original box pews, pulpit and altar rail. *(Author's collection)*

St Mary's Church, Handsworth, *c.* 1905. The chancel, north chapel and the lower part of the tower date from the thirteenth century but most of the rest is nineteenth-century. The octagonal tower top and spire were added in 1825, the north aisle in 1833 and the south aisle in 1904. St Mary's was recently restored, supported by the National Lottery and the Heritage Lottery Fund. *(Chris Sharp of Old Barnsley)*

St Wilfred's Church, Hickleton, July 2001. Although mostly Perpendicular this church has a Norman chancel arch. There are monuments to the 11th Earl of Devon, the 1st Viscount Halifax and the architect George Frederick Bodley. The churchyard has a medieval cross. The lych gate has a recess which, until fairly recently, contained three skulls. Lying on the busy A635 road between Doncaster and Barnsley, Hickleton is mentioned in documents as Chiceltone and Icheltone. Today there is nothing to see of Hickleton Castle, a motte and bailey structure, which lay to the north of the village. Its existence is remembered in Castle Hill Farm and Castle Hill Fold. *(Paul T. Langley Welch)*

Opposite: The ruins of Monk Bretton Priory in an engraving of 1840. In the time of Edward the Confessor, Alric, a Saxon lord, was in possession of the manor of Cawthorne. After 1066 the lands were given to Ilbert de Lacy, but Alric remained a tenant. Alric was succeeded by his son, Swaine, who died in 1130 and was in turn succeeded by Adam Fitzswain. In 1090 Robert de Lacy, son of Ilbert de Lacy, founded the Priory of St John of Pontefract. Swaine had given the church of Silkstone and the chapel of Cawthorne, with certain lands, towards its foundation. Adam Fitzswain wished to endow a monastery of his own foundation, and to that end granted the Prior of Pontefract 'the site of the monastery to be called of the Blessed Mary Magdalene of Lund, with Bretton and Newhall and Rainesborough [Rainborough] and Linthwaite and whatever he held in Brampton and between Dearne and Staincliff as far as Meresbrook, together with the mills of Dearne and Lund etc. ' All that remains of Monk Bretton Priory, founded by Alan Fitzswain in 1153, is situated to the east of what is now the borough of Barnsley, at Cundy Cross. Originally of the Cluniac order, both priories were subservient to the Abbot of Cluny, but in 1279 an act of contumacy resulted in the monks of Bretton being excommunicated. In 1281 the monks changed their allegiance to the Benedictine order, and they remained faithful to that order until Monk Bretton Priory was dissolved by Henry VIII in 1538. *(Brian Elliott collection)*

The nineteenth-century parish church of the Ascension, Oughtibridge, *c.* 1910. *(Chris Sharp of Old Barnsley)*

Opposite, top: The ruins of Roche Abbey, 1970s. Founded in 1147, with the backing of Richard de Bully of Tickhill, Roche Abbey is one of eight Cistercian establishments in the old county of Yorkshire. During the Dissolution of the Monasteries, when the monks at Roche were dismissed in 1538, the rector of Wickersley, Michael Sherbrook, described the destruction and plundering. 'The church was the first thing that was put to spoil . . . It would have pitied the Heart to see what tearing up of the Lead there was, and plucking up of Boards, and throwing down of the Sparres . . . and all things of Price, either spoiled, carped away or defaced to the uppermost.' *(Brian Elliott collection)*

Opposite, bottom: Standing on the medieval bridge which spans the River Don, Rotherham's Bridge Chapel, dedicated to Our Lady, is one of only two that survive in the old West Riding, the other being at Wakefield. A once common feature in medieval England, there are only six surviving intact bridge chapels in the whole of England, the remainder being at St Ives (Cambridgeshire), Bradford-on-Avon, Derby and Rochester, although the latter two do not structurally form part of the bridges. The Rotherham chapel can be dated by the will of John Bokying, master at the local grammar school, who in 1483 bequeathed 3s 4d 'to the fabric of the chapel to be built on Rotherham Bridge'. Completed in 1485, it was constructed in a style to match the cruciform parish church of All Saints. After the dissolution of chantries in 1547 the chapel came under the care of the Feoffees (a board of trustees who administered land or buildings for charitable and public purposes). It returned to religious use in the 1550s then the building became dilapidated. In 1681–2 the chapel was restored as an almshouse. From 1779 until 1826 it was used as a gaol before becoming a residence in 1888, then a tobacconist's shop. The chapel was restored and re-consecrated in 1924. *(Brian Elliott collection)*

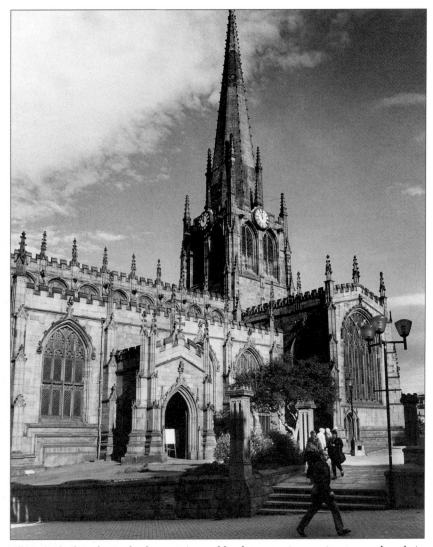

All Saints' Church, Rotherham, is arguably the most impressive town church in South Yorkshire. Standing in a commanding position overlooking the town centre, this magnificent cruciform church dates mostly from the fifteenth century. It was built largely by the monks of Rufford Abbey in the Perpendicular style. Building work began in 1409 and was financed by the sale of indulgences. Above the fan-vaulted crossing the tower and spire soar to 180ft. The nave has a particularly good panelled ceiling. The font is earlier than the main structure of the church, dating from Norman times. Furnishings include fifteenth-century stalls in the chancel and there are later medieval bench ends and screen work in the south chapel. The south chapel has been attributed to one of Rotherham's most famous sons, Thomas Rotherham, Bishop of Lincoln (later Archbishop of York), for use by the priests of his nearby College of Jesus, founded in 1482–3. The 1604 pulpit has a Georgian canopy. There is a fine organ case, the original organ being made by John Snetzler in 1777. Monuments include Elizabethan brasses, one by the mason-architect John Platt, to Mrs Buck, completed in 1752, another by John Flaxman, completed 1806 and one to fifty young men killed at the launching of a boat at nearby Masborough in 1841. There is some eighteenth-century restoration work and Victorian restoration by Sir Gilbert Scott. (*Brian Elliott collection*)

The imposing parish church of St John the Baptist, Royston, which in addition to providing a place of worship for Royston itself, once served the townships of Cudworth, Monk Bretton, Carlton, Notton, Chevet and Woolley. The church is principally fourteenth-century but the remarkably fine tower with its extremely rare pentagonal oriel window, situated between the belfry and the west window, dates from the fifteenth century. Faded wall paintings adorn the space above the chancel arch and there are Perpendicular screens in the north and south chapels. The fifteenth-century font has a Jacobean cover. Monuments include two particularly good examples to Sandford Nevile (1673) and Henry Broadhead (1754). *(Brian Elliott collection)*

A late nineteenth-century view of St Peter's Church, Sheffield's parish church. Most of the old cruciform church dates from the first half of the fifteenth century, although there are older fragments, including good stained glass, and part of a fourteenth-century Jesse window. The church was restored in the late eighteenth century and again in 1880. Raised to cathedral status in 1914, it is now known as the Cathedral Church of St Peter and St Paul. *(Author's collection)*

A late nineteenth-century postcard of St Paul's Church, Sheffield, with the newly built town hall beyond. The spire of the Catholic St Marie's Church can be seen above the roof of St Paul's. The first stone of the baroque St Paul's Church, arguably the City of Sheffield's finest Georgian building, was laid on 28 May 1720 and it was built as a chapel of ease to the nearby medieval parish church of St Peter. St Paul's, Pinstone Street, was built to the designs of Ralph Tunnicliffe of Dalton, assisted by John Platt the elder. The dome on top of the tower was added in 1769. Sheffield was an archdeaconry within the diocese of York from 1884. After the raising of the parish church to cathedral status in 1914, and owing to a shift of population from the city centre to the suburbs, many city churches became redundant. In 1936 it was decided that some had to be demolished and St Paul's was one of them. The Peace Gardens were created on the site of the church and churchyard, although the removal of human remains did not take place until the replacement Peace Gardens were laid out in 1998. (*Author's collection*)

All Saints' Church, Silkstone. The original church was built in 1090 and granted to the monks of Pontefract. Some stonework from the thirteenth-century cruciform church which replaced it survives but most of the present building is Perpendicular. The chancel was rebuilt in about 1855. Some medieval woodwork still exists in the screens and the roofs in the knave and aisles. The box pews, some bearing the owner's name, and also the pulpit date from 1835. There is a particularly fine monument to Sir Thomas Wentworth, who died in 1675, considered one of the best examples of a knight in armour of the Restoration period. There is also a memorial plaque to Joseph Bramah, engineer and machinist, who was born in the parish in 1749. In the churchyard is a memorial to twenty-six children and young adults, drowned when the nearby drift mine, known as Husker Pit, flooded following torrential rain in July 1838. Thirteen of the victims were girls. They were buried in seven graves, the girls at the feet of the boys, the oldest aged 16, the youngest 7. The Husker Pit disaster was instrumental in the Act of 1842, which stopped the employment underground of women and girls, and boys under the age of 10. *(Brian Elliott collection)*

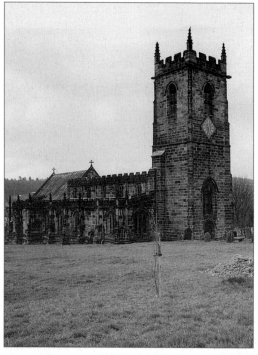

St Mary's Church, Sprotborough, *c.* 1900. St Mary's is essentially an Early English and Perpendicular church with a Decorated tower. The church contains a thirteenth-century sedilia and piscina with a credence shelf. A stone seat in the chancel, thought to date from the fourteenth century, is generally believed to be a frith-stool or 'seat of peace', placed near the altar in some churches. The frith-stool was the last refuge of those claiming sanctuary within a church. *(Chris Sharp of Old Barnsley)*

St Peter's Church, Tankersley, seen here in a 1920s Lichie Walker postcard. The church has its origins in the tenth century, although apart from two pieces of stonework nothing remains of the Saxon structure. Of more recent additions, the chancel is the oldest part of the church and dates from the early thirteenth century. The tower is Perpendicular but, with the exception of the late sixteenth-century clerestory and the north aisle, which was rebuilt in 1881, most of the rest is Decorated. Nothing exists of the medieval stained glass of which some records remain, but there is some fine stained glass in the nave. Known as the Walker windows, they were designed by Edward Burne-Jones and date from 1879. The porch, which has more ancient origins, was repaired and reconstructed in 1726 and again in 1881. The porch gate was designed by Sir Edwin Lutyens in 1901. *(Walkers Newsagents collection)*

St Mary's Church, Tickhill, *c*. 1925. This largely fourteenth- and fifteenth-century church has a tower which rises to 120ft. There is a fifteenth-century font and medieval woodwork in the pulpit and the screen to the north chapel. Some fragments of medieval glass remain; there is also some late Victorian glass by Kemp and several notable monuments, including an early sixteenth-century alabaster tomb chest with effigies of Thomas Fitzwilliam and his first wife. *(Chris Sharp of Old Barnsley)*

All Saints' Church, Wath-upon-Dearne, 1978. When South Yorkshire was divided up into parishes during the early Middle Ages the parish of Wath-upon-Dearne was created. As well as Wath itself, the parish covered Brampton Bierlow, Hoyland, Swinton and Wentworth, and also the lesser townships contained within those areas. They remained part of that parish until new parishes were created in the mid-nineteenth century. Most of All Saints' is Norman but there is some thirteenth- and early fourteenth-century work. The clerestory, the upper part of the tower and the spire are Perpendicular. *(Brian Elliott collection)*

All Saints' Church, Wath-upon-Dearne, the east window. *(Brian Elliott collection)*

All Saints' Church, Wath-upon-Dearne, the north aisle and arcade. *(Brian Elliott collection)*

Holy Trinity Church, Wentworth. Known as the New Church, building began in 1872 and the Archbishop of York consecrated the church on Tuesday 31 July 1877. Built in memory of their parents by the children of the 5th Earl Fitzwilliam, the church was designed by that great exponent of Gothic Revival, J.L. Pearson, whose work includes Truro Cathedral and Cliveden, home of the Astor family. The east window is by Clayton and Bell and was installed in memory of Countess Harriet, wife of the 6th Earl, who died in 1895. The west window is by Kempe. There are wall memorials to members of the Fitzwilliam family and to their agents.
(George Hardy collection)

Opposite, top: Holy Trinity Church, Wentworth, known as the Old Church, 1960s. Today the church is ruined except for the tower, chancel and Wentworth chapel, which comprises the south chapel, containing the chancel and north chapel (known as the Wentworth chapel) of the medieval church. Wentworth was originally part of the enormous parish of Wath-upon-Dearne. Holy Trinity Church was built as a chapel of ease in the late twelfth or early thirteenth century on land donated by the Wentworth family. Part of the church was built in the Decorated style, widely used during the fourteenth century. The incorporation of Norman elements salvaged from Monk Bretton Priory in this church has made precise dating of Holy Trinity's features difficult for architectural historians. The church contains several fine monuments to members of the Wentworth family, some to the Skiers family and a good wall monument to Sir William Rokeby and his wife Frances, who died in 1665 and 1676. The oldest monument, believed to date from the fourteenth or early fifteenth century, is situated near the position of the original altar and consists of a cross and a crossbow. Notable tombs in the ruined nave include those of members of the Townend family of Upper Hoyland Hall. *(George Hardy collection)*

Opposite, bottom: Holy Trinity Church, Wentworth. The wall monument to William 2nd Earl of Strafford and his wife the former Lady Henrietta Maria Stanley, daughter of the Earl of Derby. Both the Earl and his Countess are buried in York Minster. To the right can be seen the altar tomb to Thomas Wentworth and his wife Margaret Gascoign, great-grandparents of the 2nd Earl of Strafford. *(Paul T. Langley Welch)*

St Thomas's Church, Wincobank, *c.* 1910. The church was built in Newman Road in 1875. Its appearance belies its age, possibly because of the clever use of materials and the industrial grime that has hastened the mellowing of the stonework. Unlike many churches built throughout England during that period, St Thomas's gives the impression that it has been standing for centuries. *(Chris Sharp of Old Barnsley)*

Opposite: A Lichie Walker postcard of the interior of Holy Trinity Church, Wentworth (the New Church). *(Walkers Newsagents collection)*

All Saints' Church, Woodlands, 1920s. All Saints' was built to the design of W.H. Wood and completed in 1914. Its distinctive spire can be seen from several miles away. Woodlands, which straddles the Great North Road, was conceived on the lines of a garden village. The houses, designed by architect Percy Houlton and constructed in the fashionable Arts and Crafts style, were built to provide housing for miners and officials at nearby Brodsworth Main Colliery, sunk between 1905 and 1908 by the Stavely Coal and Iron Company. Once the largest coal mine in Britain, it closed in 1991. *(Brian Elliott collection)*

An Edwardian postcard of St Mary's Church, Worsborough. Built of local sandstone, it is an unusual-looking building, with a large, almost square, nave and aisles. St Mary's has a thin Decorated tower, with a Perpendicular top and spire. Some Norman work exists in the chancel and its arch to the nave. There is a fifteenth-century roof to the porch, which protects the very fine oak door dating from about 1480. The church also has a Perpendicular chancel screen. Several interesting monuments include that of Sir Roger Rockley, who died in 1533. There are tombs and monuments to members of the Edmunds family, who once lived at nearby Worsborough Hall, and to the Elmhirsts, a family associated with the history of this corner of South Yorkshire from at least as early as the thirteenth century. Elmhirst family members still live nearby at the historic country house Hound Hill. *(Chris Sharp of Old Barnsley)*

5

Shops, Public Houses, Inns & Hotels

Cole Brothers Ltd, Fargate, Sheffield, 1963. Founded by three brothers in 1863, the building seen here was known as Cole's Corner. The business transferred to new premises in Barker's Pool soon after this photograph was taken.
(David J. Richardson collection)

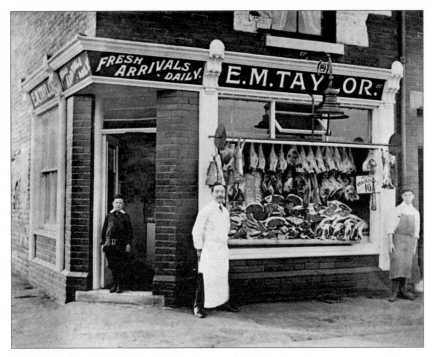

The premises of
E.M. Taylor, butcher,
Coleridge Place,
Attercliffe, 1905.
The boy standing on
the doorstep is the
young Colonel E.R.
Bradley, Commanding
Officer of the Local
Defence Volunteers
during the Second
World War. *(Sheffield
Central Library)*

John Robert Walker (1860–1929), younger son of Isaac Walker, an edge tool maker of Masbrough, Rotherham, set up in business as a wholesale and retail newsagent in the early 1880s and traded from premises in Grahams Orchard, Barnsley. This image shows his shop in about 1895. The Walker family are still trading as newsagents from two shops in Hoyland, some 7 miles from their original premises. *(Walkers Newsagents collection)*

The Old White
Bear Inn,
Shambles Street,
Barnsley,
c. 1900. It was
here that the
South Yorkshire
Miners'
Association was
formed in 1858
(see page 10).
*(Brian Elliott
collection)*

Bell Brothers, Doncaster's oldest surviving business, was established in 1781. From its original premises in French Gate, the business moved to Baxter Gate then, in the 1850s, to St Sepulchre Gate seen here in the early 1900s. The Bell family remained owners until 1938 when they sold the business to George Frampton, who retained the freehold and continued trading after his premises became part of the Arndale Centre in the 1960s. *(Author's collection)*

A 1920s photograph of the Reindeer Hotel, which stood at the Hall Gate/High Street
junction at the corner of Cleveland Street, Doncaster. The hotel is known to have existed
on the site as early as 1782; it was demolished in 1962. Note the early traffic lights.
(Author's collection)

PARKINSON'S

ESTABLISHED 1817.

The
Old
Butterscotch
Shop.

HIGH STREET,
DONCASTER.

Pastrycooks & Confectioners

ARTISTIC BRIDE CAKE MAKERS.

Sole Makers and Proprietors of the original

ROYAL DONCASTER BUTTERSCOTCH

AS SUPPLIED TO H.M. THE QUEEN AND ROYAL FAMILY.

PARKINSON'S CAFÉ

is renowned as the cosiest and most convenient in the town.

Prompt Attention and Moderate Charges.

SOLE PROPRIETORS:

S. PARKINSON & SON (Doncaster), Ltd.

ESTABLISHED 1817.

Advertisement from the Royal Horticultural Show catalogue, 1912. Samuel Parkinson opened his business in these premises at 50–1 High Street in 1817. Parkinson's butterscotch was renowned. Following a visit by Queen Victoria to Doncaster in 1851, Parkinson's supplied butterscotch to the court and royal household until closure in 1960. This Georgian building, popularly known as 'Upstairs Downstairs', was under threat of demolition. Thanks to Doncaster Civic Trust, it was saved and restored. *(Barry Crabtree collection)*

The Market, Wentworth Road, Elsecar, *c.* 1980. Formerly known as the Market Hotel, this is Elsecar's largest remaining public house. On the right can be seen the New Yard, later known as Elsecar Central Workshops. The workshops were built by the 5th Earl Fitzwilliam in 1850 to support his mining interests. They now form Elsecar Heritage Centre, officially opened by Her Majesty the Queen on 25 March 1994. *(Keith Atack collection)*

The Horseshoe Inn, Harley, which remains this small village's only public house, seen here in the early twentieth century. The couple on the doorstep are believed to be Mr and Mrs Heathcote, the landlord and landlady. *(Chris Sharp of Old Barnsley)*

The Milton Arms Hotel, Cemetery Road, Hemingfield, early twentieth century. Built during the last quarter of the nineteenth century, it was named in honour of the heir to the Fitzwilliam earldom. There have been six holders of the title Viscount Milton since the 4th Earl inherited the Wentworth estates from his uncle, the 2nd Marquess of Rockingham, in 1782. The pub was closed for several years following a murder there but reopened in the 1980s with a new name, the Fiddlers Inn. In 2001 the name was changed to the Marbrook Tavern, before reverting to its previous name in 2006. *(Chris Sharp of Old Barnsley)*

Hall's shop, 35 King Street, Hoyland, *c.* 1914. George Hall was a potato merchant who became a greengrocer and fruiterer. He and his wife Edna had sixteen children, many of whom set up greengrocery businesses themselves. The two older girls on the doorstep are Doreen and Edna Hall. The Hall family traded from these premises until the shop closed in the 1970s on the retirement of Mrs Kate Marsden, George and Edna's granddaughter. The Halls still have businesses in Hoyland today. *(George Hardy collection)*

No. 28 King Street, Hoyland, seen here in 1912, when occupied by the Maypole Dairy Co. Ltd. The manager, Albert Reynolds, who ran the Maypole until he retired to Skegness during the Second World War, stands in the right foreground. This was one of Hoyland's purveyors of superior comestibles for almost sixty years. The Maypole specialised in dairy products and traded until 1971. *(Author's collection)*

Allott & Son's delivery dray, *c.* 1900. Allotts were high-class bakers and confectioners, who operated from Hoyland Common. (*Author's collection*)

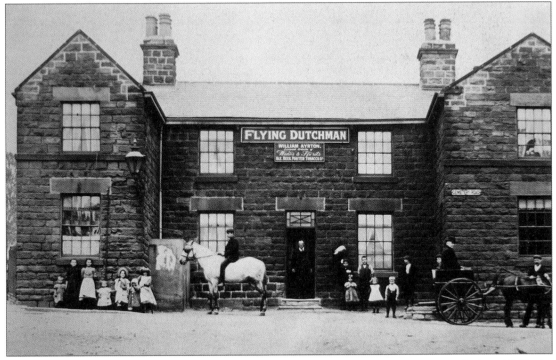

The Flying Dutchman, Jump, *c.* 1890. The village of Jump did not exist in 1830, but in 1861 the population of this new village amounted to exactly 1,000 souls. Jump was developed in Wombwell township, largely to provide housing for metal-workers in Elsecar and Milton Ironworks in Hoyland township. Evidence suggests that the Flying Dutchman was formed out of an older farm building. It has the appearance of a yeoman farmer's residence. (*Keith Hopkinson collection*)

An Edwardian view of the Millstone Inn, Tickhill. *(Author's collection)*

Ye Old Cross Scythes Hotel, Totley, seen here during the First World War. *(Chris Sharp of Old Barnsley)*

The George and Dragon Hotel, Wentworth, when John Rimes was 'mine host', early 1900s. Formerly one of Wentworth village's grander homes, the building dates from at least as early as the seventeenth century, and during the early eighteenth century it was being used as an inn. The Pepper family was closely associated with the George and Dragon during the eighteenth and nineteenth centuries. The part of the building to the right, known as the 'Court House', is thought to be where the manorial courts were held. *(Sandra Hague collection)*

High Street, Wombwell, 1920s. On the left is Jabez Lodge & Sons, newsagents, next to it is Harold Fisher's confectionery shop and beyond it the Maypole Dairy. *(Brian Elliott collection)*

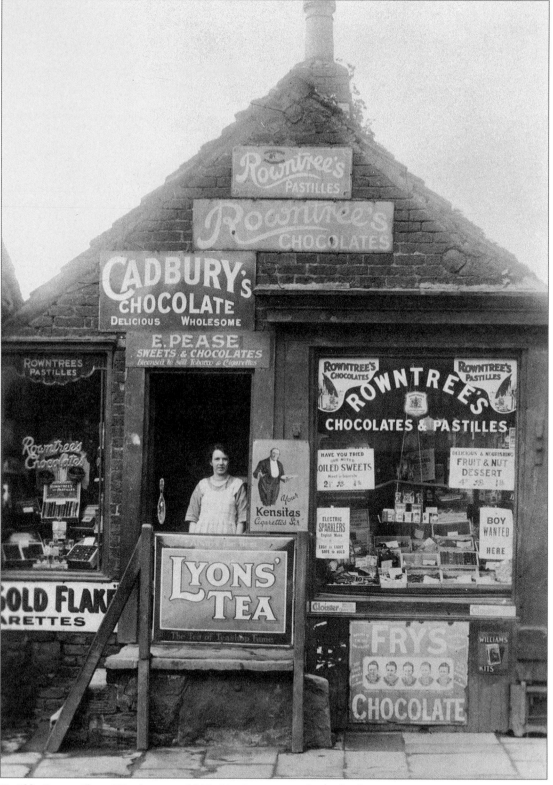

Ye Olde Sweete Shop, Woodseats, *c.* 1900. Mrs Pearce stands on the doorstep. *(Sheffield Central Library)*

6

Monuments, Follies & Curiosities

Park Well House, Rockley, *c.* 1900. *(Chris Thawley collection)*

A 1920s postcard of the Italianate observation tower in Barnsley's Locke Park. The tower was commissioned and funded by Sarah McCreery, as a memorial to her late sister Phoebe, widow of Joseph Locke, who gifted it to the town in 1877. The architect was R. Renee Spiers and the local building firm of Robinson and Son undertook the construction. *(Author's collection)*

The statue of the distinguished railway engineer Joseph Locke (1805–60), Locke Park, Barnsley, sculpted by the Italian Baron Marochetti and unveiled in 1879. *(Author's collection)*

The Roundhouse at Barrow stands in Mill Lane on the ridge above Barrow Field, between Wentworth and Harley. This former windmill was constructed in 1793 using materials from an earlier windmill, which stood in Wentworth village and was demolished that same year. The earliest mention of a windmill in Wentworth is recorded in 1590. The Roundhouse at Barrow was the last wind-powered mill to operate on Earl Fitzwilliam's Wentworth Estate and ceased work in 1835. It is now a private residence and is seen here in about 1930. *(Author's collection)*

Hoober Stand takes its name from the hamlet of Hoober and the hill where it is situated. Its base stands 518ft above sea level and it was built to commemorate the suppression of the 1745 Jacobite Rebellion. A marble tablet above the doorway has this inscription: '1748. This Pyramidall Building was Erected by His MAJESTY'S most Dutyfull Subject THOMAS, Marquess of Rockingham etc. In Grateful respect to the Preserver of our Religion Laws and Libertys KING GEORGE the Second. Who, by the Blessing of God, having subdued a most Unnatural Rebellion in Britain Anno 1746 Maintains the Balance of Power and Settles a Just and Honourable Peace in Europe 1748.' Henry Flitcroft was engaged as architect and in Hoober Stand he strayed from the rigid Palladian correctness of his other work, creating a unique sloping three-sided structure. Work started in 1747 and was completed in 1749. Hoober Stand is an 80ft high sloping pyramid ending in a corbelled parapet. Crowning this is a hexagonal domed cupola rising to 90ft, positioned directly above the central staircase. There are sundials in each corner of the platform. Five round-arched and pedimented windows light the staircase. The base measures 42ft, and 155 steps wind their way up to the top. This is one of England's most extraordinary buildings, a monumental masterpiece. From a distance it is majestic, but close up, Flitcroft's breathtaking design gives you the impression that tons of masonry are about to fall on your head. From any angle the domed cupola appears to be off-centre, again because of Flitcroft's tricks with symmetery. A complete restoration was undertaken in 1999. *(George Hardy collection)*

Hoyland Law Stand, seen here in about 1905, takes its name from Hoyland Law (or Lowe) Hill. It is the highest point in Hoyland, rising to almost 600ft, and also the highest point between Hoyland and the east coast. Built as a hunting lodge by the 1st Marquess of Rockingham, it was completed in 1750, the year in which he died. It later became a private residence until, in 1924, the Dearne Valley Water acquired the site, since when the building has gradually deteriorated. *(Author's collection)*

The Barber Fields Cupola Tollhouse, Ringinglow, *c.* 1910. Generally known as the Round House, it was built in 1791 on a site where the 1758 turnpike road from Sheffield diverged to Fox House and Chapel-en-le-Frith. It is in fact not round but octagonal, allowing those inside good views over the three roads it once collected tolls for travelling along. The Tollhouse was converted into a dwelling in 1821, having been redundant from about 1812, after the A625 road from Banner Cross to Fox House was made. *(Author's collection)*

Boston Castle, seen here as depicted in John Guest's *Historic Notices of Rotherham* (1877), was built on land belonging to the 3rd Earl of Effingham on the south-western outskirts of Rotherham at one of the highest points in the area. Construction began in 1773, but the building, conceived as a simple Gothic folly to be used as a hunting box, took on a more elaborate form when the Earl decided to mark his opposition to his country's attempts to crush the American Revolution in 1775 by highlighting the incident known as the Boston Tea Party, in which tea was thrown into Boston harbour in protest against taxation. It became a commodious two-storey structure, with a well-appointed interior, its exterior battlemented and ornamented with Gothic pinnacles. The Earl would allow no tea to be drunk at Boston Castle, because of the building's dedication. Today Boston Castle is a private residence but it can be seen at close quarters from the public park surrounding it, which was formally opened in 1876. *(Author's collection)*

The 2nd Earl of Strafford (of the second creation, not the family at Wentworth Woodhouse but a branch that revived the extinct title at nearby Wentworth Castle) decided to build what would be the last of the large structures outside the park that surrounded Wentworth Castle. Rockley Woodhouse was built in 1747 in an embayment of Friar Tail Wood, south of the Serpentine beyond Rockley Dam. Constructed in a vaguely Adamesque style it consisted of a curved arcade, with a bay-fronted room at each end and a tower in the centre, surmounted by a cupola, bearing a weather vane. Originally used as a retreat for shooting parties, or as a place to rest while on a ramble through the estate, it ended its days used mainly by fishing parties. During open-cast mining in the 1950s Rockley Woodhouse was demolished when a substantial part of Friar Tail Wood was destroyed – as was most of Green Spring Wood. This 1920s view by Roy Colville was produced as a postcard by Lichie Walker. *(Walkers Newsagents collection)*

Keppel's Column, Scholes, early 1900s. Situated on a hill above Scholes Coppice, this giant Tuscan column was conceived as an ornament to mark the southern edge of Wentworth Park, by the 2nd Marquess of Rockingham. Several designs were proposed and the Marquess kept changing his mind from conception to completion. Work began in 1773 on 'Scholes Pyramid'. He then decided on a tower and obelisk and in 1776 finally opted for a column. John Carr eventually took charge of the project but was perplexed when Lord Rockingham asked him to curtail the height of the column (which was 75ft at the time) and finish it off as quickly as possible. This he did, and instead of the intended 150ft – the correct height for the column's entatis (or curve) – the column stands at 115ft, the minimum needed to preserve the curve and finish it off neatly. However, this noticeable re-alignment causes the column to bulge and remains a talking point for passers by. The column has a viewing platform surrounded by iron railings. There are 217 steps, lit by 21 small staircase windows. The Marquess wanted to give the column political significance. The impetus to complete it came when his friend and political ally Admiral Viscount Keppel (1725–86) was court-martialled, on a charge of misconduct and neglect of duty. Lord Rockingham threw his weight behind Keppel's defence and when he was acquitted, on 11 February 1779, there were great celebrations. The column was named in Keppel's honour. *(George Hardy collection)*

The Lady's Folly in Tankersley Park, *c.* 1930. The folly was built as a retreat for Mary, Marchioness of Rockingham, by Charles, the 2nd Marquess, in about 1763, to the designs of John Carr, assisted by the master mason-architect John Platt II. A two-storey building, it was constructed in the style of a Roman temple, with a pyramidal roof and three arches on the north and south façades of the upper storey separated by attached Tuscan columns. Its isolated position on the vast estate surrounding Wentworth Woodhouse and its proximity to the heavy industry in Tankersley Park during and after the Industrial Revolution made the Lady's Folly less attractive to its owners, the Fitzwilliam family, who preferred to visit or celebrate important events at other follies on their estate. The structure became severely dilapidated and by 1960 it was considered dangerous. In those less conservation-minded times, and with so many buildings in surrounding districts being demolished because of subsidence caused by mining, the Lady's Folly was not deemed worthy of restoration and the structure was dismantled. Some of the dressed stone was used at Glebe Farm, Tankersley, and there is a popularly held belief that much of the Lady's Folly lies in storage and could be used to reconstruct this fondly remembered landmark. A stone memorial now stands on the site to record the building's existence. *(Author's collection)*

An Edwardian view of the 'Cain and Abel' statue situated in the Old Park on the Wentworth Castle Estate at Stainborough. The residents of Wentworth Castle were fond of statuary, obelisks and follies. Cain and Abel, as this much-lauded statue was known locally, was made of lead. In fact the two male figures wrestling represented Hercules and Antaeus. In the photograph it can be seen that one figure has an arm missing and by the 1940s the statue was reported to be much damaged and vandalised. Articles in the *Barnsley Chronicle* in 1951 mention the statue's disappearance and the suspicion that it had been stolen. *(Chris Thawley collection)*

The Obelisk on the Wentworth Castle Estate at Stainborough to the memory of the Rt Hon Lady Mary Wortley Montague. In 1717 Lady Mary, wife of the British Ambassador in Constantinople, returned to England. She had already had her infant son inoculated with the smallpox virus before her return. In England she had her 5-year-old daughter inoculated in the presence of several physicians, who noticed the mildness of the attack of smallpox that followed. Smallpox was a major killer, particularly of children, and Lady Mary's bold act laid the foundations for an inoculation programme that was widely implemented later in the century. *(Brian Elliott collection)*

An inscription reads:

TO THE MEMORY OF THE
RT. HON. LADY MARY
WORTLEY MONTAGUE
WHO IN THE YEAR 1720
INTRODUCED INNOCULATION
OF THE SMALLPOX
INTO ENGLAND FROM TURKEY

Stainborough Castle. This mock fortification was built on the Wentworth Castle Estate by the lst Earl of Strafford (1672–1739), on the hill which gave Stainborough its name. Lord Strafford wanted to create the illusion that his branch of the Wentworth family had been living on the estate for centuries, instead of as recently as 1708. Stainborough Castle is shown here in the early twentieth century. (*Bob Dale collection*)

Opposite: The Mausoleum, Nether Haugh, also known as the Rockingham Mausoleum, was built by William 4th Earl Fitzwilliam, in memory of his uncle, the 2nd Marquess of Rockingham, who is buried in York Minster. This monument could more accurately be described as a cenotaph ('empty tomb'). John Carr was appointed as architect to design and build the monument. Building began in 1784 and took four years to complete. Of the several designs Carr offered for consideration, one resembling the Roman tomb of the Julii at St Remy in Provence was chosen. Carr created a three-storey building some 90ft high. The ground floor is a solid square structure, built of ashlar blocks in the local sandstone. It has a pedimented entrance supported by two columns of the Tuscan order. Above is an open colonnade, supported by Corinthian columns, which contains an empty sarcophagus. The entire structure is surmounted by a cupola resembling a Roman temple. Four large vases decorated with veined and carved leaves are sited at the corners of the penultimate storey. The Mausoleum was enclosed by a fence of 743 railings made by the Rotherham iron founders Samuel Walker and in 1792 four 50ft high obelisks were removed from the lawns of the West Front of Wentworth Woodhouse, and placed within the enclosure. (*Author's collection*)

This statue of Charles Watson-Wentworth, 2nd Marquess of Rockingham, by Joseph Nollekens is in the ground-floor chamber of the Mausoleum. On the base is an inscription in prose by Edmund Burke and in verse by Frederick Montagu. There are also eight busts of Rockingham's 'Whig' luminaries placed in niches. The originals have been removed for safe-keeping and replaced by plaster casts. The busts are of Edmund Burke, Charles James Fox, Admiral Viscount Keppel, John Lee, Lord John Cavendish, the Duke of Portland, Frederick Montagu and Sir George Saville. *(George Hardy collection)*

Below: The Vinegar Stone or Stump Cross is situated on the Fitzwilliam (Wentworth) Estates in the area known as Stump Cross, between Lee Wood and Rainborough Park. It is less than 3ft high, although it may have once had a more elaborate form, having been referred to as the Stump Cross since the early eighteenth century. In common with other such monuments, its purpose may have been associated with the plague. Usually such crosses were situated near village or parish boundaries. Goods were left nearby and payment was made at the stone itself. The carved-out hollow at the top of the stone was filled with vinegar and coins were left in it. This was believed to provide protection against the 'Black Death', and there was certainly cause for concern, as the parish register of the parish of Wath-upon-Dearne, in which Wentworth fell, shows that fifty-nine people died in an outbreak which lasted from 27 June to 5 October 1646. *(Author's collection)*

The Needle's Eye, situated in Lee Wood, tops a ridge about two-thirds of a mile from Wentworth Woodhouse. The first known documentary mention of this monument is in 1723 and a visual representation of it, exactly as it looks today, appears in a 1728 engraving by Cole. The Needle's Eye is a 45ft high pyramid pierced by a Gothic ogee arch, constructed of ashlar blocks hewn from local sandstone and surmounted by a large ornamental urn. A stone seat is built into one of the walls inside the arch. Various legends surround the monument's origins, usually concerning a bet that a horse and carriage could be driven through the eye of a needle. *(George Hardy collection)*

The Roundhouse (also known as Saxon Tower) is one of two surviving former windmills on the present day Fitzwilliam (Wentworth) Estates, built close to an earlier windmill, which was taken down in 1793 and rebuilt at Barrow (see page 109). In the same year Anthony Boulby, a bricklayer, was paid £1 15s for 'converting the old windmill into a cottage called Saxon Tower'. It is built of slender handmade bricks and has a castellated top. The house in the foreground is 45 Clayfields Lane, one-time home to the Austin family. Giles Austin was appointed Farm Bailiff by the 6th Earl Fitzwilliam at Wentworth Home Farm. His second son, Herbert, was educated at the village school before going to Rotherham Grammar School. This former Wentworth resident did not follow in his father's footsteps but went on to develop what became one of the most famous marques in British motoring history. Before establishing the Austin Motor Company Ltd, Herbert Austin (1866–1941), created Baron Austin in 1936, was general manager of the Wolseley Tool and Motor Car Company Ltd. *(Paul T. Langley Welch)*

There are various accounts of the origin of the Bear Pit, which now forms an interesting attraction in today's Wentworth Garden Centre, situated in what were once the private grounds beside the West Front of Wentworth Woodhouse. It may be that the Bear Pit existed in the seventeenth century and was modified later; Watson and Pritchett, architects to the 4th Earl Fitzwilliam, are believed to have carried out some work on it. The Bear Pit is built on two levels, with two entrances. It comprises a viewing platform with a stone staircase and iron balustrade, descending to the lower vault, which contains two retiring chambers for the bears. The bottom entrance, seen here, which leads to the main chamber via a corridor, re-uses one of the original seventeenth-century Jacobean entrances to the mansion. *(Paul T. Langley Welch)*

The Rose Garden, Wentworth Woodhouse. In the centre background is the Ionic Temple, situated at the end of the 1500ft Great South Terrace, which runs from that point to the East Front of the mansion. This view was produced as a postcard in the 1920s by Lichie Walker. This is a first-generation print from the original glass slide. *(Walkers Newsagents collection)*

7

Country Houses

The original Aston Hall was destroyed by fire on Christmas Day 1771. The present building,
designed by the architect John Carr in 1772 and now a hotel, is seen here in the 1980s.
(Brian Elliott collection)

Carbrook Hall, Attercliffe Common, seen here in 1999. In the late twelfth century the Blunts lived at Carbrook. During the late Middle Ages a fine timber-framed house was erected and a new stone wing was added in 1623, by which time a branch of the illustrious Bright family of Whirlow Hall was in residence at Carbrook. During the siege of Sheffield Castle in 1644 the Parliamentarians used Carbrook Hall. The Brights accumulated vast wealth and considerable lands. Mary Bright, daughter of Thomas Bright of Carbrook Hall, married Charles, 2nd Marquess of Rockingham, of Wentworth Woodhouse, who was twice prime minister. The fortune to which Mary Bright was heiress and her pedigree had made her a suitable candidate for Lord Rockingham's hand. A descendant of the Bright's, Admiral Southerton, sold the Carbrook Hall Estate in 1819, the timber portion of the hall having been demolished in about 1800. The surrounding farmland was rapidly being engulfed by the spread of steelworks and by 1855 Carbrook Hall had become a public house. *(Paul T. Langley Welch)*

Barnburgh Hall, seen here in this nineteenth-century engraving, was originally a small manor house that was enlarged by its owners, the Cresacre family, in the early Tudor period. Various alterations took place over the centuries. The hall was demolished in the 1960s. *(Brian Elliott collection)*

Birthwaite Hall. This largely seventeenth-century hall with later additions was one time associated with the Sylvester family. John Sylvester, who lived at Birthwaite from about 1675, became a noted iron maker and was appointed Smith to the Tower of London. He forged a chain to span the River Thames, in order to repel the Dutch fleet. He died in 1722 and has an impressive memorial in All Saints' Church, Darton. From 1827 the Beaumont family lived at Birthwaite, and later the Fountain family, who had mining and quarrying interests. *(Brian Elliott collection)*

Beauchief Hall was built by Edward Pegge in 1671, on the estate owned by the Strelley family from 1573. It passed through marriage in 1648 to the Pegges and, with a change of name to Pegge-Burnell, the family remained in residence until 1909, when the snuff manufacturer William Wilson III, of Sharrow Mills, bought the hall and it became his family home. Since the 1950s the hall has been used as a hotel and for corporate gatherings. This image, viewed from the south side and taken from a lantern slide, shows the hall in about 1900. *(Sheffield Central Library)*

A 1930s aerial view of Rainborough Grange, in Brampton Bierlow, close to its border with Hoyland township. Substantial buildings existed here for over 900 years, from before the time when the monks of Monk Bretton Priory, founded in 1153, established a grange at Rainborough on land given by Adam Fitzswain. The first Rainborough Grange was built at the head of a field known as the Starbank, situated close to Rainborough Park, from stone quarried on its own estate, which involved adapting a substantial building that predated the Domesday Survey. The Rainborough Grange that replaced it, seen here, probably dates from the sixteenth or early seventeenth century and was built further down the hill some 25yds from the quarry that provided the stone for all the buildings on the estate. Rainborough Grange (a grange is simply a country house with farm buildings attached) can be seen in the middle of the photograph, on the extreme left. The quarry is out of view, behind the main house and slightly to the left, where there was a sheer drop into the deep workings. After the Dissolution of the Monasteries (1538) Monk Bretton Priory's various estates passed to new owners. The Rainborough Grange estate eventually came under the ownership of the Wentworth family of Wentworth Woodhouse. Opencast mining, which took place nearby in 1943, mostly destroyed the natural springs, causing drainage problems on the Rainborough Grange estate, making the land difficult to farm. The estate remained in the hands of the owners of the Wentworth Fitzwilliam family at Wentworth Woodhouse, and was last farmed by the Cooke family until the 1960s. Then, amid fears that the pit tip belonging to nearby Elsecar Main Colliery might subside, Rainborough Grange and part of its estate were sold to the National Coal Board. It was decided to extend the tip and secure its extremities. The entire site seen in this image was covered over by colliery waste in 1967, creating an ugly purple and grey slag heap. Today the former pit tip is clad in a luscious green blanket, and Rainborough Grange, with all its history, lies beneath. With the closure of collieries throughout the area, the site is once again in the ownership of the Fitzwilliam (Wentworth) Estates. *(Courtesy of George W. Cooke and Mrs Kathleen M. Robinson)*

Rainborough Lodge, seen from Smithy Bridge Lane, early 1900s. Also known as the Lion Gate and more commonly as 'Lions Lodge', this marks the entrance to Rainborough Park, and was built for William, 4th Earl Fitzwilliam, to the designs of John Carr in about 1796. There are in fact two separate residences which flank the gates. *(Author's collection)*

Banks Hall, Cawthorne. This fine early Georgian house was home to the Green family in the eighteenth century. It was later occupied by Samuel Thorpe, who had coal-mining interests. Banks Hall has also served as Dower House to the Spencer family of Cannon Hall. *(Brian Elliott collection)*

Cannon Hall, Cawthorne, ancestral home of the Spencer family, was built on the site of an earlier building. By the end of the thirteenth century the estate, in the manor of Cawthorne, was owned by the Canun family, from which the name Cannon Hall probably derives, and a century later ownership passed to the Bosvilles of Ardsley. In 1650 a yeoman farmer, John Hartley, bought the estate which he bequeathed to his daughter on his death in 1656. She sold the Cannon Hall Estate to her mother's second husband, John Spencer, who bequeathed it to his son, William, who in turn passed it on to his son John, who decided to landscape the park in 1761 and, in 1765, to alter the house. Richard Woods undertook the landscaping of the park, assisted by John Spencer's own gardener, Thomas Peach. In 1764 he received 'the Plan and Elevation for my house from Mr Carr'. John Carr remodelled the old house in three phases in accordance with Spencer's requirements. John Spencer was described in 1760 as 'a gentleman of modest means'. Cannon Hall is built of local carboniferous sandstone. It is a fine house, albeit somewhat plain, often described as a lesser country house of the Georgian age. Cannon Hall was bought by the County Borough of Barnsley in 1951. It is now a country house museum. (*Author's collection*)

The Drawing Room at Cannon Hall, *c.* 1965. (*Brian Elliott collection*)

Cusworth Hall, seen here in 1990, was commissioned by William Wrightson and begun in the early 1740s by the Thrybergh master-mason architect George Platt, whose son John completed the work between 1743 and 1745. The South Front, seen here, was refaced in the 1750s by James Paine, who added the flanking pavilions which served as a chapel and a library. The grounds were landscaped by Richard Woods of Chertsey, Surrey, who had landscaped the park at Cannon Hall. *(Brian Elliott collection)*

Cranford Hall, Darfield, as this substantial country house has been known since 1946, stands on the site of a medieval hall, once the seat of the Bosvile family. The old hall was replaced in the eighteenth century by a large house, which had additions during the nineteenth and twentieth centuries – when it was still known as New Hall. The house was renamed Cranford Hall by its then owner Ida Mai Wood. *(Brian Elliott collection)*

Middlewood Hall, Darfield, seen here from its attractive park in a 1905 postcard, when it was the seat of the Taylor family, who had both landed and business interests including mining and railways. The substantial country house was built in the seventeenth century on the site of a medieval hall. It was greatly altered during the Georgian period and there are some later features. In the 1980s Middlewood Hall was divided into several separate residences. *(Brian Elliott collection)*

Darton Hall, seen in this early 1900s postcard, was largely a seventeenth-century house situated in a prominent position within the village of Darton. It was demolished during the period of wholesale destruction of fine properties in the 1960s and 1970s. A housing development replaced it. *(Brian Elliott collection)*

Firbeck Hall, seen here in the 1980s, is situated in the village of Firbeck. Its estate bounded that of Park Hill, one-time home of Colonel Anthony St Leger (1727–88), after whom the great classic horse race was named. Park Hill was demolished in 1935, although the original stables, brewery and some cottages survive. The owner of Firbeck Hall in the mid-sixteenth century was William West, Chief Steward of the Manor of Sheffield, when Mary Queen of Scots was held captive there. He was an eminent lawyer and accomplished writer. In 1935 the hall became a fashionable country club, with a swimming pool and aerodrome. The Prince of Wales flew in for a visit not long after it opened and the club was frequented by the fashionable and famous. Firbeck Hall was used as a hospital during the Second World War, then as a miners' rehabilitation centre, before the NHS took it over. *(Brian Elliott collection)*

The east facing range of Hickleton Hall on an early 1900s postcard. The old mansion at Hickleton was owned by the baronet Sir John Jackson in 1673. The estate was acquired by Godfrey Wentworth, who in about 1730 built a new mansion there, to the south of the old Hickleton Palace which was allowed to go to ruin. Hickleton Hall, enlarged in about 1775, stands next to St Wilfred's Church and commands extensive views to the west. It was the home of the 1st Viscount Halifax (created 1866), whose monument is in St Wilfred's Church. By 1935 Hickleton Hall's attraction to the Wood family had diminished. In 1944 Edward Frederick Lindley Wood, Viscount Halifax and Baron Irwin, formerly Viceroy of India, became the 1st Earl of Halifax. In the late 1940s Hickleton Hall was acquired by an Anglo-Catholic sisterhood, the Sisters of the Order of the Holy Paraclete, and used as a boarding and day school for girls until 1960. In 1961 it was taken over as a Sue Ryder Home for European stateless persons. *(Author's collection)*

Hoober House, seen here in 2001, was built in the early nineteenth century to serve as the Dower House on Earl Fitzwilliam's Wentworth Estate, but it was never used for the purpose of accommodating a widowed countess. The 4th (first Earl Fitzwilliam to reside at Wentworth), 5th and 6th Earls were all predeceased by their wives. Maud, Countess Fitzwilliam, was widowed during the Second World War, when the Wentworth Estate was in turmoil because much of Wentworth Woodhouse, the stable block and several principal buildings, was being used for military purposes. Following the death of her husband the 7th Earl, in 1943, she took over the home of her son Viscount Milton and his wife, the Grange, on the Fitzwilliam's Malton Estate, where she lived until her death in 1967. Olive, Countess Fitzwilliam, widow of the 8th Earl, who died in a plane crash in 1948, lived at Coollattin House on the Fitzwilliam's Irish Estate until her death in 1977. The 9th Earl left no widow and on the death of the 10th and last Earl Fitzwilliam, who died at Wentworth Woodhouse on 21 September 1979, his widow, Countess Joyce, lived at Milton Hall near Peterborough, the Fitzwilliam's ancestral home since 1593. She died in 1995. The widowed Laura, Viscountess Milton, also lived there until her death in 1886. *(Author's collection)*

The Hauslin family lived in Harley and Wentworth for nearly four centuries and were one-time residents of Harley Hall. Situated on Dyke Hill, it was recorded in 1587 as Harley Hall, the Grange of Hoyland, one of the possessions of Thomas Wentworth of Wentworth Woodhouse. At the time it was a timber-framed house. The original timber structure, of which a few fragments remain, was gradually enlarged and rebuilt in the local sandstone, a feature of many buildings in the area. Harley Hall and its adjacent cottages and outbuildings lay just within the Hoyland township until 1938, when boundary changes occurred. The hall and its complex of buildings are seen here in April 1967. *(Author's collection)*

Situated in Old Hellaby Lane, off the A31 (Bawtry) road, between Rotherham and Maltby, Hellaby Hall, seen here in 1997, was threatened with demolition a decade earlier, having deteriorated after a fire in 1976 destroyed most of the interior. Fortunately a local construction company bought the hall and restored it with the help of English Heritage. Hellaby Hall was built for a local man Ralph Fretwell, a Quaker, who made his fortune planting sugar in Barbados. He returned to Hellaby in 1688 and work began on the hall, which was built from Roche stone and inspired by Dutch merchants' houses he had seen in Barbados. After restoration Hellaby Hall became part of a hotel complex. *(Brian Elliott collection)*

Hoyland Hall, arguably the finest of Hoyland's few remaining Georgian buildings, *c.* 1920. Its elegant proportions have been masked by early 1990s additions, but these have been constructed in a style that complements the original building. Hoyland Hall may have been constructed on the site of an earlier hall, as a Hoyland Hall is mentioned in documents dating back to 1579, but this might be another building that still exists in Upper Hoyland, which plainly has older origins and is known today as Upper Hoyland Hall. It is not known for whom the hall was built, and its architect is also unknown but it is built in a similar style to houses designed by John Carr and John Platt II. The field in which Hoyland Hall was built was named in 1771 as the Fork Royds. The Hoyland Enclosure Commissioners referred to 'the gardens of this messuage as the garden or pleasure ground of Samuel Phipps and Ann Reresby'. Perhaps these were the first owners of the hall.

    In 1814 W.N. Parker, manager of Earl Fitzwilliam's short-lived tar distillery at Elsecar, was living at Hoyland Hall. In 1822 James Green, described as a sheriff's officer, gave his address as Hoyland Hall. Shortly after this, Henry Hartop, a partner in the Milton Ironworks who later ran Elsecar Ironworks for Lord Fitzwilliam, took up residence there and remained until 1841. Three separate deeds, of 1837, 1838 and 1839, concern an estate of 102 acres in Hoyland and Worsborough. They cover the sale of land by the Earl of Mulgrave, of Mulgrave Castle, to William Vizard, of Lincoln's Inn Fields, who took up occupancy after his tenant, Henry Hartop, left. William Vizard came from a distinguished legal family. He became the first owner of the Hoyland Silkstone Colliery and also acquired additional land. The Hoyland Hall Estate remained in the hands of his family for more than forty years. William Vizard died at Little Faringdon, Berkshire, in 1859 aged 84. His son, also called William, inherited but he died in 1865, and the estate passed to his brother the Revd Henry Brougham Vizard, who died aged 49 in 1874, when the estate passed to his son Harry William Vizard of Portland Place, Lyme Regis – its last Vizard owner. He put the estate up for sale in 1884. During the twentieth century Hoyland Hall was largely occupied by high-ranking mining officials, and after it ceased to be a private residence was used for educational purposes, before standing empty for several years. Extended, Hoyland Hall now serves as a residential home for the elderly. (*Walkers Newsagents collection*)

Manor Farm, Hoyland, sometimes referred to as Manor House Farm, seen here in about 1930, was one of Hoyland township's principal residences and was believed to have been built in the form seen here mainly during the seventeenth century. In about 1747 a Mr Johnson came to live there, after which Methodist preachers often stayed at Manor Farm, which caused quite a stir throughout the area. John Wesley preached from the nearby Tithe Lane steps in 1772. In 1809 William Gray, the then resident at Manor Farm, donated land on which Hoyland's first Methodist church, St Paul's, was built in 1809. Manorial Courts were sometimes held at Manor Farm, whose land, like several other farms in central Hoyland, became engulfed by housing developments in the mid-twentieth century. Manor Way, which follows the path of the original cart track to the house across Nether Field, was built during the late 1940s, the houses there being first occupied in 1950. With insufficient land to work the house was no longer a viable residence and Manor Farm was demolished in June 1957. *(Author's collection)*

Ouselthwaite Hall. This attractive smaller country house, seen here in this early twentieth-century postcard, is situated in a commanding position overlooking Worsborough Country Park, Stainborough and Wentworth Castle. This is a largely seventeenth-century hall, with eighteenth- and nineteenth-century additions. For many years the hall was associated with the Elmhirst family, the main branch of which still reside nearby at Hound Hill. Ouselthwaite Hall is now divided into apartments. *(Brian Elliott collection)*

Rockley Old Hall is situated in the area now known as Worsborough Country Park; an area of outstanding natural and managed beauty on the outskirts of Worsborough village. Once a grand mansion and home to the distinguished Rockley family, Rockley Hall is seen here in the early twentieth century, after its role as a home for the gentry had been downgraded and it had become just another farmhouse, in need of repair. Now generally referred to as Rockley Old Hall, the major portion of this many-gabled country house dates from the sixteenth century. It continued to be used as a farmhouse until it was divided into several separate dwellings in the 1970s. Occupants have included footballing legend Jack Charlton, during his tenure as manager of Sheffield Wednesday, and the actress Kathy Staff, best known for her TV appearances in *Crossroads*, *Open All Hours* and the long-running *Last of the Summer Wine*, in which her character Nora Batty became one of the most popular on British television. *(Chris Sharp of Old Barnsley)*

The East Front of Sandbeck Hall, *c.* 1985. This building replaced an earlier hall constructed in about 1626. James Paine rebuilt it for 4th Earl of Scarbrough and worked at Sandbeck from about 1762 to 1770. The hall was built in the Palladian style in magnesium sandstone. Its magnificent park was landscaped by Lancelot 'Capability' Brown, who completed it in 1780. (*Brian Elliott collection*)

This early postcard shows Bishop's House, situated in Meersbrook Park, Norton Lees Lane, about 2 miles south of Sheffield city centre. This fine example of a prosperous yeoman's residence dates from the late fifteenth century and has sixteenth- and seventeenth-century additions. It is the earliest timber-framed house still standing in Sheffield. The east wing contains the hall, kitchen and a small chamber. Additional rooms are provided in the cross wing added in about 1550. For many years the Blythe family were associated with Bishop's House. After extensive renovation the house was opened as a museum in 1976. (*Author's collection*)

An early twentieth-century view of the sixteenth-century Turret House, Manor Castle. This is the only part of the once extensive Manor Lodge, one-time seat of the earls of Shrewsbury and place of incarceration of Mary Queen of Scots, to survive intact. The top floor chamber has a fine plaster ceiling, and the arms of the Talbot family, the family name of the earls of Shrewsbury, are displayed over the fireplace. (*Author's collection*)

The Skiers family takes its name from the hamlet situated within Hoyland's boundaries. Skiers Hall, seen here during the 1920s long after it had been converted into cottages, dated from the fourteenth century, when, as well as living at Skiers Hall, members of the Skiers family were also living at nearby Alderthwaite, once a hamlet but today simply a large farm. The Skiers family owned the Skiers Hall estate throughout the medieval period. In 1555 the Rokeby family took up residence, until the main line became extinct in 1678. The hall then passed to the Veney family for a brief period. William, 2nd Earl of Strafford of Wentworth Woodhouse, then bought the estate, and on his death in 1693 bequeathed it to Robert Monckton. Skiers Hall was a substantial residence with sixteen hearths recorded on the Hearth Tax Roll of 1672. Shortly before his death in 1750 the 1st Marquess of Rockingham, a descendant of Lord Strafford, bought the Skiers Hall estate from Viscount Galway (a Monckton), and it has remained in the hands of his descendants ever since. Unfortunately, the hall itself was demolished in 1951. This 1920s postcard was published as one of a large series of South Yorkshire views by Lichie Walker, a Hoyland confectioner and newsagent, with photography by Roy Colville. (*Walkers Newsagents collection*)

Sprotborough Hall was home to the Copley family from 1516 until it was sold in 1925. It was demolished shortly afterwards, its own stones being used to fill the basement. The site was then levelled and a housing estate built. *(Brian Elliott collection)*

An early twentieth-century postcard of Ivanhoe Cottage, Sprotborough. Sir Walter Scott stayed here while he was working on his novel *Ivanhoe*, set in nearby Conisborough Castle. This rather attractive country house has now become the Boat Inn. *(Chris Sharp of Old Barnsley)*

Opposite: The ruins of Tankersley Old Hall, 1940s. In about 1546 the Saville family built Tankersley Lodge, which soon became known as Tankersley Hall. Situated within Tankersley Park, this became the principal mansion on the Tankersley estate, and the former mansion of the Savilles became a farm, eventually demolished and replaced by another. The Savilles sold the estate, then in 1631 Viscount Wentworth (later the 1st Earl of Strafford) purchased it from Philip, Earl of Pembroke, for £4,500. It has remained in the ownership of the Wentworth Estate, now known as the Fitzwilliam (Wentworth) Estates. Lord Wentworth paid the hall less attention than its previous owners, preferring to reside at his ancestral seat Wentworth Woodhouse, situated 2 miles to the east. The Civil War erupted in 1642, and a minor battle took place nearby when the Earl of Newcastle's Royalists met enemy forces numbering about 2,000 on Tankersley Moor.

The Royalists won the day and many Roundheads were slain or taken prisoner. The Earl's efforts on the King's behalf during the Civil War resulted in his advancement, first to Marquess and later to Duke of Newcastle. The hall's last recorded occupants were Sir Richard Fanshaw and his family. Sir Richard's occupancy came about because of his connection with the Wentworth family. In 1640 he was made Secretary to the Council of War under the 1st Earl of Strafford in Ireland. In 1644 he became Secretary of War under the Prince of Wales, then aged 14. While Sir Richard was on business for the Prince in Paris, Charles 1 was executed. Sir Richard remained loyal to the Royalist cause and fought in the Battle of Worcester (3 September 1651), where he was wounded and taken prisoner. He was incarcerated in the Tower of London before being moved to Whitehall, where he was kept under close arrest.

He was seriously ill and in 1653 was bailed for £4,000 in order to receive medical treatment in Bath. That winter he visited his friend William, 2nd Earl of Strafford, at Wentworth Woodhouse. Lord Strafford offered him Tankersley Hall as a temporary residence, and Sir Richard took a twenty-one-year lease on Tankersley Park. He moved there with Lady Fanshaw and their three children in 1654. On parole, he was not permitted to travel more than 5 miles from his new home without special leave. However, the Fanshaw family's stay at Tankersley did not last long. In 1654 Sir Richard's daughter, Ann, contracted smallpox and died. She was buried in the nearby St Peter's Church. Overcome with grief, Sir Richard and Lady Fanshaw were unable to settle at Tankersley Hall and went to stay with Lady Fanshaw's sister at Hamerton, Huntingdonshire. The Fanshaws' lease indicated that Lord Strafford was contemplating the extraction of coal and iron ore in and around Tankersley Park, including the erection of 'Iron Mills'.

In a picture dated between 1723 and 1728 Tankersley Hall is shown intact, with its outbuildings in good condition and with red deer in the Deer Park. Daniel Defoe visited Tankersley Park in 1727, and stated that these deer were the biggest in Europe. Some time between then and 1772, when a survey was conducted for the 2nd Marquess of Rockingham, which showed that both coal and ironstone had been worked to within a field's length of the hall, the hall became sufficiently dilapidated to be described as a ruin. The mansion was partially demolished to provide building stone for use elsewhere on the Wentworth Estate. Fireplaces can still be seen in place on the interior walls. In the film *Kes*, based on *A Kestrel for a Knave* by locally born author Barry Hines, the ruins of the Old Hall were chosen as the location in which the character Billy Casper (played by David Bradley, later known as Dai Bradley) scaled the walls to take a young kestrel from its nest. (*Author's collection*)

Thundercliffe Grange, seen here in about 1903, was built near Tinsley in 1776–83 by the master-mason architect John Platt II for Thomas Howard, 3rd Earl of Effingham (1747–91). The attic storey was added some time after Platt's work had been completed. Once situated in splendid isolation, Thundercliffe Grange, now a series of luxury apartments, nestles closer to the Ml motorway than any other such fine country house throughout its entire length. *(Brian Elliott collection)*

A Scrivens postcard of the grounds of Tickhill Castle, early twentieth century. Richard I licensed tournaments at Tickhill, when a simple wooden motte and bailey structure existed, dating from William the Conqueror's reign. During his absence on the Crusades his brother John seized the castle in 1191. When John became King in 1199 he spent over £300 on the castle defences. During 1321 and 1322 the Earl of Lancaster tried to call a Parliament at Doncaster. Civil war followed and in February 1322 Tickhill was besieged for three weeks. In 1540 John Leland, the traveller, described Tickhill as 'very bare' but its church was 'fair and large'. It is said that Oliver Cromwell remarked during the storming of Tickhill Castle in 1664, 'Tickhill, God help them', before the Royalist stronghold fell under Roundhead control. The Castle was dismantled in 1648. Only the gatehouse survives and a few fragments of the original structure. The mansion seen here is believed to have been built in the castle grounds by the Hansby family towards the end of the sixteenth century. Tickhill Castle is owned by Her Majesty the Queen and is part of the Duchy of Lancaster. *(Brian Elliott collection)*

Wadworth Hall was built for the Wordsworth family in about 1748. If not wholly his original design, Wadworth was completed by James Paine. In the 1930s it became home to the Cooke-Yarborough family. In more recent years this fine house has been used as an old people's home and for corporate purposes. (*Brian Elliott collection*)

Warmsworth Hall was largely rebuilt in 1702, incorporating parts of an earlier manor house principally forming the present east wing. One of the hall's most famous occupants was Colonel Anthony St Leger, tenant for a brief period during the late eighteenth century. It now forms part of a hotel. (*Brian Elliott collection*)

Wentworth Castle, Stainborough, *c.* 1970, showing the east-facing Baroque range by Jean de Bodt. The building was modelled around Stainborough Hall, which survives at the rear. John Plat II worked on the south-facing Palladian range to the left. Lord Raby, who had inherited the junior title of the 2nd Earl of Strafford of Wentworth Woodhouse, but not the estates, purchased the property in 1708. By 1731 the enlarged mansion had been provocatively renamed Wentworth Castle, to cock a snook at the 'usurper' who lived 6 miles away at Wentworth Woodhouse. (*Author's collection*)

Wentworth Woodhouse, the East Front, seen here in this early twentieth-century postcard, when William Charles de Meuron, 7th Earl Fitzwilliam, was its owner. At 606ft in length, this front is the longest of any country house in England. (A full description appears on page 142.) *(Author's collection)*

The West Front of Wentworth Woodhouse was constructed around an earlier house dating from about 1630, built by Thomas Wentworth, lst Earl of Strafford, which itself had been constructed around the old Wentworth ancestral mansion. Work was carried out on this substantial Baroque range in 1725–8 but even before completion plans were afoot to build an east-facing range of gargantuan proportions. Its builder, Thomas Watson-Wentworth, had inherited the house from his father the Hon. Thomas Watson-Wentworth, known locally as 'His Honour Wentworth', who died in 1723. Thomas Watson-Wentworth was created Knight of the Bath in 1725, a fact commemorated in the heraldic device at the centre of the West Front. In 1728 he was elevated to the peerage, becoming Baron Malton. Then in 1733 he was created Baron Harrowden, Viscount Higham and Earl of Malton. Meanwhile, work continued in the house, which had been fully fitted out by 1734, and was well underway on the foundations of the new additions to the east. The architect of the Baroque West Front is not known. It has no rivals in England, being more akin to buildings found in Austria or Bohemia. During this period the name of the house was changed to Wentworth House, which it remained until the time of the 4th Earl Fitzwilliam, who lived there from 1782 to 1833, when the house reverted to its old name. As work continued on the great house Lord Malton consulted the Earl of Burlington, considered the arbiter of fashion at that time, who recommended Henry Flitcroft (known as 'Burlington's Harry') as a suitable architect for the work. Lord Malton was persuaded that the heroic Vanbrughian style he had set his sights on was already out of date. Instead, Lord Burlington suggested Colen Campbell's Wanstead House, designed for Sir Richard Childe in 1715, as the model on which to base the design. Flitcroft designed the nineteen-bay central portion of the East Front in the Palladian style, closely resembling Wanstead House, allowing his resident architect Ralph Tunicliffe of Dalton to carry out work on the north and south wings. This new front was 606ft long. Flitcroft also designed the pavilions. Wentworth Woodhouse is effectively two massive houses built back to back to make one palatial mansion – the largest private house in the United Kingdom, which it remains today. A massive 1,500ft terrace was constructed with a bastion at the east end. During the years that followed many fine craftsman carried out work on the interior. Henry Flitcroft's most important contribution was the fitting out of seven rooms on the *piano nobile*, including his finest work, the Marble Saloon. Joseph Rose (senior), the plasterer, worked extensively in the house. After Lord Rockingham's death on 14 December 1750, his fifth and only surviving son, Charles, inherited the estate. Twice Prime Minister, the 2nd Marquess continued to build on the estate. He employed John Carr to build a stable block large enough to accommodate eighty-four horses. Work began in 1766. On Lord Rockingham's death in 1782, his heir was his nephew, William, 4th Earl Fitzwilliam, son of his sister, who inherited his uncle's estates with an income of £40,000 a year. Between 1782 and 1784 John Carr designed alterations to Tunnicliffe's wings, adding an additional storey. This very early postcard of the West Front (also known as the Garden Front or colloquially as the 'Back Front') shows the original alignment of the principal façade of the mansion that has graced this site in ever-increasing size over many centuries. *(Author's collection)*

Cortworth House, Wentworth, seen here in the 1990s, was built beside the area known as Glasshouse Green on Earl Fitzwilliam's Wentworth Estate by the 6th Earl during the last half of the nineteenth century. He built it as a home for his land agent and brother-in-law, Admiral the Hon. Henry Douglas, a younger son of the 17th Earl of Morton, Lord Fitzwilliam's wife's father. The interior of the house was sumptuously appointed and the house served as the residence to successive land agents of the estate until the tragically early death, by a wasp sting, of Guy Canby, on Bradfield Moor in August 2004. The present agent chose to live in a more modest home than the ten-bedroom Cortworth House. The house, its extensive outbuildings and attractive gardens have since been rented to a private tenant. *(Author's collection)*

Worsborough Hall, seen here in this early twentieth-century postcard, was built for the Edmunds family in the early seventeenth century and extended in the Georgian period. There are notable tombs to the family in nearby St Mary's Church. Thomas Edmund, a staunch Royalist, was one-time secretary to the Great Earl of Strafford. The main branch of the Edmunds continued to live there until the 1830s. Later that century Worsborough became home to several colliery owners. It was bought by the National Coal Board, before being sold and divided into apartments. *(Brian Elliott collection)*

ACKNOWLEDGEMENTS

My thanks to Iris Ackroyd, Keith Atack, Vera Atack, Joan Bostwick, Arthur K. Clayton (1901–2002), Barry Crabtree, R.A. (Bob) Dale, Iris J. Deller, Joanna C. Murray Deller, Ricky S. Deller, Tracy P. Deller, Brian Elliott, Simon Fletcher, Margaret Gaddass, George Hardy, Doug Hindmarch (Senior Local Studies Librarian at Sheffield Central Library), Keith Hopkinson, Ann Howse, Doreen Howse, Kathleen Howse, Jane Hutchings, Peter Marsh (1936–2004), Eleanor Nelder, Stanley Nelder, David J. Richardson, Cyril Slinn, Chris Thawley, Michelle Tilling, David and Christine Walker (of Walkers Newsagents, Hoyland), Adam R. Walker, Anna Walker, Darren J. Walker, Ivan P. Walker, Paula L. Walker, Suki B. Walker, Bow Watkinson, Clifford Willoughby, Margaret Willoughby, Roy Young. I am particularly grateful to John D. Murray, who has assisted me over many years.

A twentieth-century Scrivens postcard of Doncaster Racecourse. (*Brian Elliott collection*)